# Le Creuset's

# A TASTE OF
# EUROPE

*Le Creuset's*

# A TASTE OF
# EUROPE

## OVER 150 AUTHENTIC RECIPES

### THE SCOTTO SISTERS

MARTIN BOOKS

**Design:** Patrick McLeavey & Partners

**Photography:** Sue Atkinson

**Styling:** Andrea Lambton

**Food preparation for photography:** Joanna Farrow

**Illustration:** Hilary Downing

**Additional cover photographs:** Ace Photo Agency/Duncan Davies

**English translation:** Carole Fahy in association with First Edition Translations Ltd, Cambridge UK

**Typesetting:** Andrew Wilson in association with First Edition Translations Ltd, Cambridge UK

Printed and bound in Great Britain by Butler & Tanner Ltd, Frome and London

Published by Martin Books
Simon & Schuster Consumer Group
Grafton House  64 Maids Causeway
Cambridge CB5 8DD

in association with
The Kitchenware Merchants Ltd
4 Stephenson Close
East Portway  Andover
Hampshire  SP10 3RU

With thanks to Sue Cutts, home economist for Le Creuset

First published 1992
© 1992 The Kitchenware Merchants Ltd
ISBN 0 85941 809 X

## RECIPE NOTES

All measures are level. All eggs are medium (size 3) unless otherwise stated. Measurements are given in both metric and imperial measures; use either set of quantities, but not a mixture of both, in any one recipe.

# CONTENTS

# FOREWORD

The European Community brings to us all an opportunity to explore the heritage, language and life-styles of our European partners – and to explore a wealth of wonderful cuisines. As travelling in Europe – for business or pleasure – increases, it is likely that this most enjoyable aspect of cultural exploration is already well underway. By bringing together the first twelve Community countries in this European cookery book, Le Creuset have chosen to illustrate the styles of cookery each country has to offer. Some dishes are well known, others not so, but each has the combination of a little history; local produce and that 'certain something' indigenous to the people who created it.

Like so many of these dishes, Le Creuset cast-iron cookware has been used for centuries and its cooking qualities are famous. Nothing beats Le Creuset in evenness of cooking and energy-efficiency – once hot it maintains its heat on the lowest of settings. And Le Creuset can be used on all kinds of hobs and in all kinds of conventional ovens.

Le Creuset is supremely suited to innumerable cooking tasks and fits in well in the most basic of kitchens, or the most technically advanced. Cast-iron is one of the few materials naturally suited to the revolutionary glass-topped induction hob, but works just as well on the simplest of gas rings.

Delicate sauces can be cooked to perfection over a gentle heat, whilst sugars can be turned to golden caramel at a higher temperature. Pastry will be crisp and golden baked in cast-iron, and meat will remain moist and tender in the renowned lidded cocotte.

The extensive range of shapes available means that there is one to suit almost any recipe; the Scotto sisters have had no difficulty in choosing shapes in which to prepare any of the recipes in this book, whatever the country of origin.

A gratin dish is as well suited to cook *Daurade à la Provençale* from France as it is to bake a delicious apple pie from Great Britain. In Europe the casserole, or cocotte as it is better known, is used much more as a hob cooking pot rather than in the oven and this is reflected in the recipes which appear in these pages.

Some of the more unusual Le Creuset shapes are also used. The marmitout (a lidded casserole whose upturned lid serves as a skillet or frying-pan); a steamer that sits neatly over a casserole base; a buffet casserole that is wide and shallow and ideally suited to cooking rice, fish and vegetables – the list is endless. Because colour co-ordination in the kitchen is important, the existing range of colours Le Creuset offers is reflected in the photography.

Most of these recipes are not 'haute cuisine', but they are central to the culinary traditions of their country of origin. We hope they are dishes you will enjoy trying, safe in the knowledge that elsewhere in Europe they have been enjoyed by families and their friends for centuries.

No book can encapsulate the whole of European cuisine but, as its title implies, we hope this one will give you that 'taste of Europe' that will whet your appetite for more.

*Bon Appétit!* From Le Creuset.

# INTRODUCTION

The European Community is still in the process of being built although it is taking great strides forward now. National borders are opening up and Europeans are becoming closer economically and politically. Will this spell the end of national identities within Europe? Happily not, since a cultural identity relies on so much more than the way a country is governed: it is above political systems and closer to the everyday life in which it evolves minute by minute. Gastronomy – regional or national – is an integral part of that culture and a modern European cookery book bears witness to the immense riches of our developing Community and to the fact that the term union is not synonymous with uniformity.

By exploring national cuisines, this book sets out to be a guide and introduction to the many facets of the European love of food – a vast and fascinating subject. As Europe becomes a genuine area of free exchange, a Dutchman will find it easy to obtain the ingredients for an Italian dish or a Greek to make a British one.

In the course of this gastronomic tour we hope to give our readers the opportunity to discover the tastes and eating habits of their closest neighbours and the desire to venture further afield and participate in the discovery of Europe's great culinary inheritance.

*The Scotto Sisters*
*June 1992*

# FRANCE

## *IF THE SCENT OF ITALY IS THAT OF BASIL,*
## *France's must be that of the bouquet garni,*

whose origins are lost in a thousand country hot-pots. But France is not just the home of simmering stews. Its culinary range is vast and differs enormously from one region to another. The rough climate of the north, the gentle winds of the south, with the Atlantic on the west coast and the Mediterranean to the south, have cut France into four, culinarily speaking. And French cuisine has two distinct faces: in the north it is a cuisine of butter and wonderful potato and cabbage dishes of all kinds; in the south – where olive oil reigns to the east and groundnut oil to the west – vegetables come into their own in a heavenly kaleidoscope of bright colours and heady flavours. The smell and flavour of the dishes change too, depending on where they are cooked: the cuisine of Calais is quite different from that of Nice, of Strasbourg from that of Toulouse and of Bordeaux from that of Lyon. In Paris, however, the whole gamut of French cooking can be found, as well as its own rich and varied cuisine of the Ile de France. The latter may be thought of as the archetypal French cuisine, with its overtones of perfection, elegance and subtlety,

but it is not representative of French cooking as a whole. *Blanquettes* and *navarins*, *daubes* and *bouillabaisses*, *bourrides* and *confits d'oie*, *choucroutes* and *foies gras*, *aligots* and *potées*, *aïolis* and *cassoulets* – none of these originate in the Ile de France but come from the four corners of a land with a richly turbulent gastronomic history.

In the Middle Ages the French ate meat stews, moistened with the juice of unripe fruit and seasoned with spices brought back from the crusades. The Renaissance saw the development of dishes made with sugar: fruit in sugar, almond paste, pastries and those sweetmeats brought from Italy by Catherine de Medici when, with her pastry cooks in attendance, she came to France to marry the future king Henry II.

Louis XIV was responsible for giving a great boost to French gastronomy. He introduced new vegetables such as cardoons, cauliflowers and peas. He also brought tea, coffee and chocolate into fashion in France. His cooks were appointed *officiers de bouche* (officers of the royal mouth). Culinary taste became more and more refined up until the nineteenth century, at which point, unfortunately, only the most grand, complicated and convoluted dishes were considered worthy of note.

From the Middle Ages to the present day, innumerable cookery books by master chefs, from Taillevant to Escoffier and from Pierre de Lune to Carême, the most imaginative of all, have borne witness to the evolution of this cuisine. And now the twentieth century marks the return in France to simple and natural food and the virtues of regional cooking. Today culinary France is a mosaic of provinces, each of which is giving new life to its own cuisine by promoting its traditional recipes and indigenous cheeses and wines. And, in the process, creating new evidence for future generations of the genius of French cooking.

# SOUPE AUX POIREAUX ET AUX POMMES DE TERRE

## *Leek and Potato Soup*

### SERVES 4

*300 g/10 oz leeks, white part only*
*300 g/10 oz firm potatoes, e.g. King Edwards*
*25 g/1 oz butter*
*1 litre/1 ¾ pints water*
*6 pinches grated nutmeg*
*100 ml/3½ fl oz whipping cream, chilled*
*4 sprigs chervil*
*salt*

1 Trim, wash and drain the leeks and chop them. Peel, wash, drain and finely dice the potatoes.

2 Melt the butter in a large saucepan and sweat the leek and potato in this for 5 minutes on a very low heat. Add the water, season with salt, cover the pan and leave the soup to cook for 30 minutes on a low heat.

3 At the end of this time, blend the soup in a food processor or blender. Pour it back into the saucepan, add the nutmeg and heat it through.

4 Whip the cream until it clings to the whisk and fold it into the soup. Remove the chervil leaves from their stems, sprinkle them over the soup and serve immediately.

# OEUFS COCOTTE A LA CREME DE TOMATE

## *Egg Ramekins with Tomato Sauce*

### SERVES 4

*750 g/1½ lb just ripe tomatoes*
*3 small onions*
*25 g/1 oz butter*
*2 pinches grated nutmeg*
*2 pinches caster sugar*
*150 g/5 oz thick* crème fraîche *or 150 ml/¼ pint double cream .*
*8 eggs*
*4 tarragon leaves*
*salt and pepper*

1 Scald the tomatoes in boiling water for 10 seconds, cool them under cold running water, remove the skins, halve and de-seed them. Finely dice the flesh. Chop the onions very finely.

2 Melt the butter in a medium-size saucepan. Put in the onions and allow them to cook on a low heat for 5 minutes until they turn golden, turning them all the time with a wooden spatula.

3 Add the tomatoes to the pan and allow them to cook for 5 minutes. Add the salt, pepper, nutmeg and sugar and pour in the cream. Stir the sauce for another 3 minutes and then remove from the heat.

4 Preheat the oven to Gas Mark 8/230°C/450°F. Put 2 dessertspoons of the tomato sauce in the bottom of each of 4 large individual ramekins. Make a well in the centre of each.

5 Break the eggs two by two into a bowl and slide them in turn into the ramekin wells. Wash and dry the tarragon leaves, chop and sprinkle them over the eggs. Coat the eggs with the remaining tomato sauce. Cover the ramekins with lids or tinfoil.

6 Fill a baking dish with hot water and sit the ramekins in this; the water should come up to within 1 cm/½ inch of the rims. Transfer the tin to the oven and cook the eggs for 10 minutes.

7 Remove the ramekins from the oven and place them on individual plates, decorated with a small folded serviette. Serve immediately with fingers of toast and butter.

# SOUPE AU PISTOU

## Vegetable Soup with Basil Sauce

SERVES 6

*200 g/7 oz dried haricot beans, soaked for 8 hours*
*125 g/4 oz runner beans*
*250 g/8 oz small courgettes*
*250 g/8 oz firm potatoes, e.g. King Edwards*
*250 g/8 oz just ripe tomatoes*
*2 garlic cloves*
*1 sprig basil*
*100 g/3½ oz pasta, e.g. small shell shapes, chopped
macaroni, etc.*
*salt*

For the *pistou*:
*250 g/8 oz just ripe tomatoes*
*4 garlic cloves*
*1 large bunch basil (100 g/3½ oz)*
*100 ml/3½ fl oz virgin olive oil*
*2 pinches salt*

For the garnish:
*100 g/3½ oz Emmental or parmesan cheese, grated
finely and freshly*

1  Drain the haricot beans. Put them in a large
cocotte, cover them well with water and cook them
for 1 hour. Drain and discard any remaining cooking water.

2  Meanwhile, string and slice the runner beans;
rinse and dry them. Wash the courgettes and cut
off the ends. Cut each courgette in quarters lengthwise and then into 1 cm/½-inch fan shapes. Peel
and wash the potatoes and cut them into 1 cm/½-
inch cubes.

3  Scald the tomatoes in boiling water for 10 seconds, cool them under cold running water and
remove the skins. Cut them in half, de-seed them
and roughly chop the flesh. Bruise the garlic cloves
slightly, but keep them whole.

4  Add the vegetables, garlic cloves and basil to the
cocotte with the haricot beans and fill it with cold
water to cover them completely. Bring the soup to
the boil slowly over a low heat. Season it with salt,
cover the pan and leave it to simmer for 1 hour.

5  Meanwhile, prepare the *pistou*: scald the tomatoes for 10 seconds in boiling water, cool them

under cold running water, remove the skins, cut
them in half and de-seed. Roughly chop the flesh
and leave to drain in a colander. Cut the garlic
cloves into quarters. Wash and dry the basil, retain
the leaves and throw away the stalks.

6  When the soup is cooked, remove the bruised
garlic cloves and sprig of basil. Add the pasta and
leave to cook for a few minutes longer, until the
pasta is tender.

7  Meanwhile, put all the *pistou* ingredients – drained
tomato, basil leaves, garlic, olive oil and salt – into
a food processor bowl. Blend just long enough to
obtain a purée that is not too smooth.

8  When the pasta is cooked, transfer the soup to a
tureen. Add the *pistou* to it, mix and serve immediately. The cheese should be handed round separately.

# BAGNA CAUDA

## Anchovy Paste

SERVES 6

*12 salted anchovies (2 x 50 g/2 oz tins)*
*4 garlic cloves*
*75 g/3 oz butter*
*4 tablespoons virgin olive oil*

For the garnish:
*French bread, sliced and toasted*
*crudités, e.g. celery, cauliflower, radish, fennel,
artichoke seasoned with pepper, red or green peppers,
etc.*

1  Rinse the anchovies under cold running water,
rubbing well to remove all the salt. Separate them
into individual fillets, removing the heads and
bones. Cut each fillet into small pieces.

2  Crush the garlic cloves and place them in a small
saucepan. Add the anchovies, butter and olive oil.
Stir over a low heat until a smooth paste is obtained.

3  Serve immediately, on the toasted French bread,
or as a dip for a variety of crudités.

# PIPERADE

SERVES 6

*2 large red peppers*
*2 large green peppers*
*2 onions*
*1 kg/2 lb just ripe tomatoes*
*2 garlic cloves*
*1 fresh chilli, red or green*
*4 tablespoons olive oil*
*1 pinch caster sugar*
*6 eggs*
*6 slices York ham, 3 mm/⅛ inch thick*
*salt and pepper*

**1** Set the grill to medium. Wash and dry the peppers and place them under it, not too close to the heat, and leave them for about 20 minutes, turning frequently, until the skins turn black.

**2** Meanwhile, chop the onions finely. Scald the tomatoes in boiling water for 10 seconds, cool them under cold water, peel and de-seed them and roughly chop the flesh. Chop the garlic finely. Wash, halve, de-seed and roughly chop the chilli.

**3** When the peppers are cooked, place them in a bowl. Cover and leave to cool. Remove the stems and any burnt pieces of skin. Halve the peppers, de-seed them and remove the white pith. Slice them into strips about 1 cm/½ inch wide.

**4** Heat 3 tablespoons of the olive oil in a large frying pan or buffet casserole. Soften the onions in this for 5 minutes until transparent, stirring all the time. Add the garlic, chilli and peppers and stir together for a further 5 minutes. Add the tomatoes, sugar, salt and pepper and mix well. Cover and leave to cook on a low heat for 30 minutes, stirring from time to time.

**5** At the end of this time, break the eggs into a bowl, season and beat them with a fork. Pour them into the pan and mix just enough to bind all the ingredients together. Keep the piperade hot.

**6** Heat the remaining oil in another frying pan and lightly brown the slices of ham in this, for about 30 seconds each side.

**7** Turn the piperade out into a deep dish, arrange the slices of ham around it and serve immediately.

# TERRINE DE CANARD

## *Duck Terrine*

SERVES 6

*1 x 1.5 kg/3½ lb duck, preferably Barbary duckling*
*250 g/8 oz unsmoked lean bacon*
*1 onion*
*2 garlic cloves*
*25 g/1 oz butter*
*40 g/1½ oz pistachio nuts, peeled*
*200 ml/7 fl oz aspic jelly, made with Madeira*
*3 level tablespoons chopped parsley*
*1 teaspoon fine sea salt*
*1 teaspoon freshly ground pepper*
*1 piece barding fat, to fit the terrine*

**1** Ask your butcher to skin and bone out the duckling. Put the duck meat and the bacon through a mincer. If you have the duck liver, clean and mince it with the other meat.

**2** Preheat the oven to Gas Mark 2/150°C/300°F. Chop the onion and garlic cloves very finely. Melt the butter in a small pan and sauté the onion and garlic in this until they turn golden. Turn them into a large bowl to cool.

**3** Add the minced meats, pistachio nuts, aspic jelly, parsley, salt and pepper to the bowl. Mix well.

**4** Line a 1.2 litre/2 pint rectangular pâté terrine with the barding fat. Turn the contents of the bowl into this and smooth the surface with the back of a spoon. Put the lid on the terrine and place it in a bain-marie or large shallow pan, such as a roasting tin, filled with hot water to within 2.5 cm/1 inch of the top. Transfer the terrine to the oven and leave it to cook for 1 hour.

**5** At the end of this time, take the lid off the terrine and continue to cook for a further 45 minutes. If the water in the bain-marie evaporates too quickly, add hot water to it as necessary.

**6** When the duck terrine is cooked, remove it from the oven and allow it to cool before putting it in the refrigerator. Leave the terrine to stand for at least 12 hours before serving.

**7** Serve the terrine at room temperature, sliced and accompanied by gherkins, onions, pickled cherries, toast and a seasonal salad.

# FRANCE

Bouillabaisse
*(Provençal-style Fish Stew)*

Mouclade
*(Mussels in White Wine and Herbs)*

Maquereaux aux Vin Blanc
*(Mackerel in White Wine)*

# BOUILLABAISSE

## *Provençal-style Fish Stew*

SERVES 6-8

*3 kg/7 lb fresh mixed Mediterranean fish and shellfish, e.g. rascasse (scorpion fish), John Dory, monkfish, conger eel, weever fish, sea bass, red mullet, cuttlefish, sole, brill, crab, lobster, crayfish*
*500 g/1 lb ripe tomatoes*
*2 carrots*
*1 leek*
*1 celery stick*
*1 onion*
*4 dessertspoons olive oil*
*1 sprig dried thyme or 1 small sprig fresh thyme*
*1 sprig dried rosemary or 1 small sprig fresh rosemary*
*1 sprig dried fennel or 1 small sprig fresh fennel*
*1 bay leaf*
*1 strip dried zest of orange*
*6 garlic cloves*
*10 parsley stalks*
*6 pinches saffron threads*
*500 ml/18 fl oz dry white wine*
*500 ml/18 fl oz water*
*salt and pepper*

To serve:
*slices of toasted French bread*
*garlic cloves*

1 Ask the fishmonger to scale the fish, remove the heads and gut and clean them, reserving the heads and bones. Cut the larger fish into 4 cm/1½-inch slices and leave the others whole. Wash them and wipe dry. If you are including crayfish or lobster, split them in half and separate the head and tail; discard the sac from the head. Clean the cuttlefish, keeping only the tentacles and the body; wash it and wipe dry.

2 Wash and roughly chop the tomatoes. Peel the carrots and leek and wash them, together with the celery. Mince the onion, celery and leek finely, including the tender green part of the latter. Cut the carrots into thin slices.

3 Heat the olive oil in a large saucepan or cocotte. Put in the bones and heads of the fish and shellfish and stir for 5 minutes over a low heat. Add the tomatoes, carrots, leek, celery and onion. Stir again for a further 5 minutes until the vegetables begin to turn golden. Add the thyme, rosemary, fennel, bay leaf, zest of orange, whole garlic cloves, parsley stalks, saffron, salt and pepper. Stir for 1 minute, then pour in the white wine and the same amount of water. Leave to simmer for 45 minutes.

4 At the end of this time, sieve out the fish heads and bones as well as the thyme, bay leaf, fennel, rosemary, parsley, garlic and orange zest. Put the rest in a food processor and blend until a smooth consistency is obtained.

5 Wipe out the pan and pour the resultant soup back in. Bring it to the boil slowly over a low heat and add the fish, beginning with the strongest fleshed (cuttlefish, eel, monkfish, scorpion fish, mullet), then add those that are more tender (weever, John Dory, sea bass, sole, brill), allowing the liquid to boil up in between the addition of each fish. Lastly, add the shellfish. Leave the soup to simmer for 10 minutes, then take out the fish and shellfish with a draining spoon and arrange them on a serving dish to keep hot.

6 Pour the soup into a tureen and serve with small pieces of bread rubbed with garlic. Serve the fish after the soup.

# LOUP AU FENOUIL

## *Sea Bass with Fennel*

SERVES 4

*1 sea bass, 1.5 kg/3½ lb*
*30 sprigs fresh fennel*
*salt and pepper*

This dish is best cooked on a barbecue. A variety of vegetables may be cooked on the barbecue at the same time, for example whole aubergines, which are then skinned and mashed with a few drops of lemon juice; courgette halves; skinned peppers, cut into strips with oil drizzled over, etc.

The dish may also be cooked in a preheated oven at Gas Mark 8/230°C/450°F, in an oval gratin dish lined with sprigs of fennel and flamed at the end of cooking in 2 dessertspoons of pastis.

1 Ask the fishmonger to gut but not skin the fish. Wash it and wipe dry. Season the fish inside and

out with salt and pepper. Place 8 sprigs of fennel in the cavity.

**2** Preheat a barbecue. When the charcoal is hot, throw on the remaining fennel so it burns and flavours the fish. Place the fish on the oiled barbecue grill over the fire and cook for 12 minutes on each side.

**3** As soon as the fish is done, arrange it on a serving dish and serve immediately.

## MAQUEREAUX AU VIN BLANC

### Mackerel in White Wine

SERVES 4

*12 small mackerel, about 100 g/3½ oz each or 6*
*medium-size mackerel (225 g/7½ oz)*
*1 onion*
*2 carrots*
*1 unwaxed lemon*
*1 bouquet garni, consisting of a bay leaf, 1 sprig*
*thyme and 6 sprigs parsley*
*500 ml/18 fl oz dry white wine, e.g. Muscadet*
*4 tablespoons white wine vinegar*
*1 dried chilli*
*2 garlic cloves*
*1 teaspoon peppercorns*
*salt*

**1** Ask the fishmonger to gut the fish. Rinse, dry and season them.

**2** Chop the onion finely. Peel and wash the carrots and cut them into very thin slices. Wash and dry the lemon and slice it very thinly. Tie up the bouquet garni ingredients.

**3** Pour the wine into a large saucepan and add the onion, carrots, lemon, vinegar, bouquet garni, dried chilli – crumbling it between your fingers – crushed garlic, peppercorns and salt. Bring the liquid to the boil and simmer for 10 minutes. Drop the fish in and simmer for a further 3 minutes (5 minutes if you are using medium-size mackerel).

**4** Take out and drain the fish and arrange them in a 1.5 litre/2½ pint terrine, alternating with the carrot, onion and lemon. Boil up the cooking liquid

for a further 5 minutes to slightly reduce it. Remove the bouquet garni and strain the resultant stock.

**5** Pour the stock over the fish and leave it to go cold. Cover the terrine and keep it in the refrigerator. Leave the mackerel to marinate for 12 hours before serving.

## FONDUE SAVOYARDE

### Cheese Fondue

In Savoy, where they love fluffy fondues, cooks often add a stiffly beaten egg white, or a pinch of bicarbonate of soda to the cooked fondue.

SERVES 4

*400 g/13 oz Emmental, beaufort or comté cheese*
*200 g/7 oz raclette cheese*
*1 French bread stick*
*1 garlic clove*
*300 ml/½ pint dry white wine (e.g. from the Savoy*
*region)*
*2 tablespoons kirsch*
*pepper*

**1** Grate the Emmental, beaufort or comté cheese, using the coarse side of the grater, and cut the raclette cheese into cubes. Cut the bread into 1 cm/ ½-inch slices, then cut each slice into quarters consisting of middle and crust parts.

**2** Rub the garlic clove around the pot of the fondue set. Pour in the wine and heat it over a medium heat on the kitchen hob. As soon as it comes to the boil, turn all the cheese into the wine, stirring well. Stirring continuously over a low heat, allow the cheese to melt until it turns to a creamy smooth, oily consistency. Add the kirsch and pepper. Stir again and then remove the pot from the heat.

**3** Put the fondue pot on to its spirit heater and bring it to the table. Each guest serves him- or herself by spearing pieces of bread and dipping them into the melted cheese. If the fondue thickens up again too quickly, thin it by adding a few spoonfuls of white wine.

# MOUCLADE

## *Mussels in White Wine and Herbs*

### SERVES 4

*2.5 kg/6 pints fresh mussels*
*300 ml/½ pint dry white wine, e.g. Muscadet, Gros Plant*
*1 sprig thyme*
*1 bay leaf*
*6 sprigs parsley*
*3 shallots*
*25 g/1 oz butter*
*1 level teaspoon curry powder*
*1 pinch chilli powder*
*100 g/3½ oz thick* crème fraîche *or 100 ml/3½ fl oz double cream*
*2 egg yolks*

1 Scrape the mussels and remove their beards. Rinse them in several lots of water and drain. Discard any mussels that are cracked or shells that are open and do not close when sharply tapped.

2 Pour the wine into a large cocotte. Add the thyme, bay leaf and parsley, bruising them well between your fingers. Put the pan on to a high heat. As soon as the wine comes to the boil, plunge in the mussels and stir with a slotted spoon. As soon as the mussels open, take them out with the draining spoon and set them aside in a bowl. Discard any that don't open.

3 On a high heat boil up the cooking liquid to reduce it by one-third, and then strain it into a bowl.

4 Meanwhile, finely chop the shallots. Melt the butter in a small saucepan and cook the shallots in this, stirring continuously, for 2 minutes until they turn golden. Add the mussel liquid and leave it to boil for 1 minute.

5 Strain the liquid back into the cocotte and add the curry powder, chilli powder and two-thirds of the cream. Boil it for 1 minute. Whisk the egg yolks in a bowl with the remaining cream. Add 2 tablespoons of the liquid from the cocotte to the bowl, whisk again and then pour it back into the cocotte. Add the mussels and heat it through, stirring, for 1 minute over a very low heat: the sauce must not be allowed to boil.

6 Divide the mussels and their sauce between 4 warm, deep plates and serve immediately.

# DAURADE A LA PROVENÇALE

## *Sea Bream Provençal-style*

### SERVES 4

*1 sea bream, 1.25 kg/3 lb*
*500 g/1 lb ripe tomatoes*
*2 garlic cloves*
*4 dessertspoons olive oil*
*1 level dessertspoon chopped parsley*
*1 unwaxed lemon*
*salt and pepper*

1 Ask the fishmonger to scale and gut the fish. Rinse it and pat dry. Season it with salt and pepper.

2 Preheat the oven to Gas Mark 8/230°C/450°F. Scald the tomatoes in boiling water for 10 seconds, cool them under cold running water, remove the skins, halve and de-seed them. Roughly chop the flesh. Finely chop the garlic cloves.

3 Heat half the olive oil in a large frying pan. Put in the garlic and parsley and cook, stirring continuously with a wooden spatula, until the garlic is lightly golden. Add the tomatoes, salt and pepper and mix well. Leave it to cook for about 5 minutes on a medium heat, until nearly all the liquid from the tomatoes has evaporated.

4 Place the bream in an oval gratin dish that is just large enough to hold it and sprinkle it with the remaining oil. Turn the fish over in the oil to coat it evenly. Cover it with the tomato sauce.

5 Wash, dry and slice the lemon thinly and arrange it over the fish. Transfer the dish to the oven. Leave the fish to cook for 25 minutes.

6 As soon as the bream is cooked, take it to the table in its gratin dish and serve immediately.

# POULET AUX QUARANTE GOUSSES D'AIL

## Chicken with Forty Cloves of Garlic

SERVES 4

*1 chicken, 1.75 kg/3½ lb*
*40 garlic cloves (about 4 heads)*
*2 sprigs fresh thyme*
*2 sprigs fresh rosemary*
*2 sprigs fresh sage*
*2 celery sticks, tender inner ones with leaves, roughly chopped*
*2 sprigs flat-leaf parsley*
*3 tablespoons olive oil*
*salt and pepper*

To serve:
*slices of wholemeal bread, toasted*

1 Ask your butcher to draw the chicken. Wash it, wipe dry and salt it inside and out.

2 Preheat the oven to Gas Mark 6/200°C/400°F. Separate the garlic cloves and remove the outer but not the inner skin. Fill the chicken cavity with half the thyme, rosemary, sage, celery, all the parsley and 4 of the garlic cloves. Place the remaining thyme, rosemary, sage and celery in a marmitout roaster or large oval casserole. Add the olive oil, salt and pepper and the remaining garlic cloves. Roll the chicken in this aromatic oil and then cover the casserole with its lid.

3 Place the casserole in the oven and leave the chicken to cook, without disturbing, for 1¾ hours.

4 At the end of this time check that the chicken is cooked. If it is, remove it from the oven and place it on a serving dish. Surround it with the browned garlic cloves. Remove the fat from the cooking juices by skimming it from the surface with a spoon or kitchen paper. Reheat the juices, and pour this gravy into a sauce-boat. If there is very little juice, add 5 tablespoons of water and boil rapidly for 1 minute.

5 Serve the chicken hot, accompanied by toast slices, and serve the sauce separately: each guest crushes his or her own garlic cloves over the toast to extract the savoury cooking juices.

# COQ AU VIN

## Chicken in Red Wine

SERVES 6

*1 cockerel or chicken, 2.5 kg/5½ lb, jointed and cut into 10 pieces*
*100 g/3½ oz smoked bacon, in one thick rasher*
*24 button mushrooms*
*1 bouquet garni, consisting of 1 bay leaf, 1 sprig thyme, 1 sprig rosemary and 8 parsley stalks*
*1 dessertspoon oil*
*50 g/2 oz butter*
*24 small flat onions*
*2 dessertspoons brandy*
*750 ml/1¼ pints Burgundy red wine*
*3 garlic cloves*
*1 teaspoon sugar*
*4 pinches grated nutmeg*
*salt and pepper*

1 Wash and wipe dry the chicken pieces. Season them. Cut the bacon into small pieces. Remove and discard the bottom part of the mushroom stalks. Wash the mushrooms and wipe dry. Tie up the bouquet garni ingredients.

2 Heat the oil and the butter in a large round casserole. Brown the whole onions, bacon and mushrooms; then take them out and set them aside.

3 Put the chicken pieces in the casserole and cook them for 10 minutes to brown on all sides. Sprinkle the brandy in and ignite it. As soon as the flame dies down, pour in the wine and add the bouquet garni, whole garlic cloves, salt, pepper, sugar and nutmeg. Stir, and when the liquid comes to the boil, cover the casserole with a lid and leave it to cook for 1½ hours, stirring from time to time.

4 At the end of this time, add the bacon, mushrooms and onions and leave to cook for a further 30 minutes.

5 When the chicken is cooked, take the pieces out of the casserole and arrange them on a serving dish. Remove the bouquet garni and boil up the sauce over a high heat for 2 minutes to thicken it. Coat the chicken with the sauce and serve immediately, accompanied by fresh pasta or boiled potatoes.

# DAUBE PROVENÇALE

## Provençal-style Stew

SERVES 6

1.25 kg/3 lb beef (skirt, braising steak or stewing steak)
4 garlic cloves
1 onion
2 cloves
1 bouquet garni, consisting of 1 sprig thyme, 1 sprig sage, 1 bay leaf, 2 celery sticks and 2 strips dried zest of orange
500 ml/18 fl oz Côtes du Rhône red wine
2 dessertspoons brandy
150 g/5 oz pork rind, fat cut off
250 g/8 oz carrots
3 dessertspoons olive oil
4 pinches grated nutmeg
200 g/7 oz belly of pork, slightly salted
200 ml/7 fl oz water
500 g/1 lb ripe tomatoes
salt and pepper

1  Cut the beef into 5 cm/2-inch cubes. Cut the garlic cloves into quarters. Stick the onion with the cloves. Tie up the bouquet garni ingredients.

2  Put the cubes of meat into a large non-metallic bowl and immerse them in the wine and brandy. Add the bouquet garni, garlic and onion, cover the bowl and leave the meat to marinate for 12 hours in the refrigerator.

3  Preheat the oven to Gas Mark 2/150°C/300°F. Cut the pork rind into 2 cm/¾-inch cubes. Blanch in boiling water for 2 minutes, then drain. Put half the pork rind into a large cocotte.

4  Peel and wash the carrots and cut them into medium thick slices. Heat the olive oil in a large frying pan. Add the carrot slices and sauté them over a high heat for 7-8 minutes until golden. Add salt and the nutmeg. Remove the carrots with a slotted spoon and set them aside on a plate.

5  Drain and wipe dry the beef, reserving the marinade. Cut the belly of pork into thin slivers. Using the cooking oil from the carrots, cook the beef and belly of pork for 5 minutes until they turn brown, stirring continuously.

6  Turn the beef and belly of pork out into the cocotte containing the pork rind and surround the meat with the carrots. Top it with the remaining pork rind and add the reserved marinade and water. Scald the tomatoes in boiling water for 10 seconds, cool them under cold running water, peel, halve and de-seed them; chop the flesh. Add them to the cocotte with the bouquet garni, garlic and onion from the marinade. Season the mixture.

7  Cover the cocotte with oiled greaseproof paper and a lid. Put it in the oven to cook for 3½-4 hours.

8  At the end of this time, take out the onion and bouquet garni. Serve the beef with the carrots, rind and belly of pork, coated with the thick, syrupy stock (reduce the stock for a few minutes over a high heat). Serve the stew with fresh pasta.

# FONDUE BOURGUIGNONNE

## Meat Fondue

SERVES 6

1.5 kg/3½ lb piece of lean beef (rump steak or fillet)
2 garlic cloves
2 sprigs thyme
2 bay leaves
2 cloves
600 ml/1 pint groundnut oil

1  Cut the beef into 2.5 cm/1-inch cubes. Wipe them and divide them between 6 small dishes.

2  Place the garlic cloves in the fondue pot with the thyme, bay leaves and cloves. Pour in the oil and heat it over a very low heat on the kitchen hob to a temperature of 180°C. At this temperature the oil begins to bubble slightly and a morsel of bread dropped into it will immediately rise to the surface.

3  Once this temperature is reached, remove the thyme, bay leaves and cloves with a slotted spoon. Move the fondue pot to its spirit heater and bring it to the table.

4  Each guest spears a piece of meat, plunges it into the oil and cooks it to taste. The meat should not be eaten straight from the fondue fork as it will be *very* hot. Transfer the meat on to a plate before dipping it in a chosen sauce: tomato, Béarnaise, *pistou*, etc. Serve with French bread and a selection of salads.

# BLANQUETTE DE VEAU

## *Veal Blanquette*

SERVES 4

*750 g/1½ lb shoulder of veal*
*500 g/1 lb tenderloin of veal*
*500 ml/18 fl oz chicken consommé or good chicken*
*stock*
*1 garlic clove*
*1 small onion*
*2 shallots*
*2 celery sticks, tender inner ones with leaves, chopped*
*in half*
*3 carrots*
*125 g/4 oz thick* crème fraîche *or 150 ml/¼ pint*
*double cream*
*2 teaspoons lemon juice*

**1** Wash the meat and wipe dry. Cut the shoulder veal into 3 cm/1-inch cubes and the tenderloin into 2 cm/¾-inch slices. Bring some water to the boil in a large saucepan and put in the pieces of meat. Bring it back to the boil and leave to cook for 1 minute; then drain the meat, rinse it and drain it again.

**2** Pour the consommé into a large round cocotte. Add the same amount of water and the veal. Add the whole garlic clove, onion and shallots to the cocotte, together with the celery. Peel the carrots, cut them into slices and add them to the cocotte. Bring the liquid to the boil slowly over a low heat and leave it to simmer covered for 1¾ hours.

**3** At the end of this time, pour the contents of the cocotte into a colander over a big saucepan. Discard the garlic, onion, shallots and celery and put the meat and carrots back into the cocotte. Cover it to keep it hot.

**4** Boil the cooking liquid rapidly over a high heat to reduce it to 200 ml/7 fl oz and remove it from the heat. Mix the cream and lemon juice together, pour them into the reduced cooking liquid and whisk for 1 minute until the sauce is thoroughly amalgamated and smooth. Pour it over the meat and heat through for 5 minutes on a very low heat. Serve immediately with fresh pasta, or with creole or pilaff rice.

# RATATOUILLE

## *Provençal-style Stewed Vegetables*

This is a light version of the dish, where the vegetables are not fried before being simmered.

SERVES 6

*500 g/1 lb courgettes*
*4 aubergines*
*1 large red pepper*
*1 large green pepper*
*3 garlic cloves*
*250 g/8 oz onions*
*400 g/13 oz just ripe tomatoes*
*200 ml/7 fl oz water*
*5 tablespoons olive oil*
*salt and pepper*

**1** Trim the ends off the courgettes and aubergines. Wash them and cut them into 2 cm/¾-inch cubes. Wash the peppers and cut them into quarters vertically, removing the stem, seeds and white pith. Cut the pieces into 2 cm/¾-inch squares.

**2** Cut the garlic cloves into fine slivers. Mince the onions finely. Scald the tomatoes in boiling water for 10 seconds, cool them under cold running water, remove the skins, halve and de-seed them; chop the flesh into small cubes.

**3** Pour the water into a large round casserole. Add the olive oil, garlic, salt and pepper. Bring it to the boil and allow it to boil for 1 minute before tipping all the vegetables into the casserole. Bring it back to the boil, cover the casserole and leave the ratatouille to cook over a medium heat for about 45 minutes, stirring from time to time. At the end of the cooking time the vegetables should be tender and there should be no water left. Serve the ratatouille hot as an accompaniment to fish, poultry, or grilled or roast meat.

# FRANCE

Fondue Bourguignonne
*(Meat Fondue)*

# FAR AUX PRUNEAUX

## *Prunes in Batter*

SERVES 6

*300 g/10 oz prunes*
*500 ml/18 fl oz milk*
*75 g/3 oz salted butter*
*125 g/4 oz plain white flour*
*125 g/4 oz caster sugar*
*5 eggs*
*2 tablespoons rum*

**1** Leave the prunes to soak overnight in a bowl of tepid water.

**2** Next day, prepare the *far* batter. Preheat the oven to Gas Mark 5/190°C/375°F. Heat the milk in a small saucepan on a low heat. Melt the butter in a second saucepan.

**3** Sieve the flour into a bowl and add the sugar. Pour the milk over this, stirring with a wooden spatula, and incorporate the eggs, one by one, the melted butter and the rum.

**4** Butter a rectangular 30 cm/12-inch oven dish. Drain the prunes and spread them in the bottom. Coat them with the batter mixture and transfer the dish to the oven. Leave the prunes to cook for about 35 minutes, until the top is golden.

**5** Remove the dish from the oven and leave it to cool. Serve the prunes warm, from the oven dish. They may be dusted with caster sugar before serving.

# CLAFOUTIS

## *Cherries in Batter*

SERVES 6

*750 g/1½ lb ripe black cherries, sweet variety*
*2 tablespoons vanilla sugar*
*4 eggs*
*150 g/5 oz caster sugar*
*125 g/4 oz plain white flour*
*2 pinches salt*
*250 ml/8 fl oz milk*

**1** Preheat the oven to Gas Mark 5/190°C/375°F. Wash and pick over the cherries, removing any stalks, but leaving the stones in. Wipe them dry. Butter a large 33 cm/13-inch oval gratin dish (the dish should be large enough to hold all the cherries in a shallow layer). Spread the cherries in this, sprinkle in the vanilla sugar and roll the cherries in it.

**2** Put the eggs into a bowl, add 125 g/4 oz of the caster sugar and beat with a balloon whisk or electric whisk until the mixture whitens.

**3** Incorporate the flour and salt, sieving them into the bowl, followed by the milk. Whisk until the batter is smooth and then pour it evenly over the cherries.

**4** Transfer the dish to the oven and leave the clafoutis to cook for 30 minutes, until it has turned golden. Dust it with the remaining caster sugar and cook for a further 5 minutes. Leave it to cool before serving in the gratin dish.

# TARTE AUX POIRES AMANDINE

## *Pear Tart with Almonds*

SERVES 6-8

For the pastry:
*50 g/2 oz butter, softened*
*1 pinch salt*
*1 egg*
*125 g/4 oz plain white flour*

For the filling:
*75 g/3 oz butter*
*75 g/3 oz ground almonds*
*75 g/3 oz crystallised sugar*
*2 tablespoons kirsch*
*2 small eggs, beaten*
*750 g/1½ lb Williams pears, red if possible*

**1** To make the pastry, put the butter in a bowl with the salt. Work them together well with a spatula for 1 minute, then add the egg and mix again for 1 minute more. Add the flour all at once and work the mixture rapidly with your fingertips until the dough forms a smooth ball: this takes no longer than 1 minute. Put it into a plastic bag and leave it to chill in the refrigerator for 30 minutes.

2 At the end of this time, make the tart. Preheat the oven to Gas Mark 7/220°C/425°F. Roll out the pastry and put it into a 24 cm/9½-inch tart dish.

3 Then make the filling. Melt the butter in a small saucepan and leave it to cool slightly. Put the ground almonds into a larger pan, add the sugar and stir the mixture well with a spatula. Pour the butter and kirsch over it, still stirring, and finally stir in the eggs.

4 Cut the pears into quarters, and peel and core them. Cut each quarter into long thin slices. Add the pear pieces to the almond mixture.

5 Turn the filling into the tart case and smooth the top with a spatula. Transfer the dish to the oven and leave the tart to cook for 40 minutes. Serve it warm.

# CREME CARAMEL

SERVES 6-8

*1 vanilla pod*
*1 litre/1 ¾ pints whole milk*
*200 g/7 oz caster sugar*
*½ teaspoon lemon juice*
*8 eggs*

1 Preheat the oven to Gas Mark 5/190°C/375°F. Split the vanilla pod in half lengthwise and put it into a saucepan with the milk. Bring it to the boil, then remove it from the heat and leave it to infuse while you prepare the caramel.

2 Prepare the caramel: put half the sugar into a small saucepan with the lemon juice and 2 tablespoons of water. Bring it to the boil and cook until an amber-coloured caramel is obtained. Remove it from the heat and pour it into a 2 litre/3½-pint charlotte mould, soufflé dish or deep cake tin, or 6–8 individual soufflé dishes.

3 Break the eggs into a large bowl and add the remaining sugar. Beat them with a balloon whisk until smooth, then add the hot milk, beating all the time. Strain the liquid through a fine conical sieve over the caramel.

4 Place the caramel mould, or moulds, in a bain-marie or large shallow pan, such as a roasting tin, filled with hot water to within 2.5 cm/1 inch of the top. Transfer this to the oven. Leave it to cook for 45 minutes to 1 hour depending on whether you are using several small moulds or one large one. The cream should have set and a knife inserted in the centre should come out cleanly.

5 Take the cream caramel out of the oven, remove it from the bain-marie and leave it to cool. It may be served at room temperature (turned out of the mould on to a dish) or cold. In the latter case, place it in the refrigerator and, when ready to serve, pop the base of the mould into hot water for 30 seconds to facilitate turning out.

# GATEAU MOELLEUX AU CHOCOLAT

## *Chocolate Gâteau*

SERVES 6

*200 g/7 oz plain cooking chocolate*
*200 g/7 oz butter, softened*
*4 eggs*
*200 g/7 oz caster sugar*

1 Preheat the oven to Gas Mark 5/190°C/375°F. Butter a deep non-stick 22 cm/8½-inch sandwich tin.

2 Break the chocolate into pieces and melt it in a bowl over a pan of hot water. Add the butter and mix with a wooden spatula until smooth.

3 Separate the eggs, reserving the whites in one bowl and the yolks in another. Add half the sugar to the yolks and whisk until the mixture whitens. Pour in the melted chocolate and whisk again.

4 Whisk the whites to a firm snow and fold in the remaining sugar, still whisking until the mixture is smooth and shiny in texture. Fold this meringue carefully into the chocolate mixture using a spatula.

5 Turn the mixture into the tin and transfer it to the oven. Cook for 40 minutes, then remove the gâteau from the oven and leave it to cool before turning it out. Serve warm, cold or chilled, with or without dark chocolate sauce or custard.

# ITALY

## ITALIAN COOKERY IS KNOWN AS THE MOTHER
### *of Mediterranean cuisine.*

It certainly gave French cooking a boost when in 1535 Catherine de Medici married Henry II. The history of gastronomy in Italy is linked to the history of the country. The Etruscans, who loved good living but whose recipes have not survived, were followed by the Romans who were soldier farmers and no gourmets. But from 270 BC, when they mastered the peninsula, the vast conquests the Romans went on to make taught them to enjoy good food. An amazing work by Apicius – the oldest known cookery book – bears witness to this. Here can be found innumerable recipes illustrating the luxury and splendour of Roman cuisine. Local produce from the sea, the hunt, stock-farming, sumptuous orchards and luxuriant gardens, all feature in this book, together with imported luxuries such as exotic fruits, spices from the Orient and truffles from Libya. The recipes themselves were refined and complex, rich, sweet and savoury: honey, muscat wine, olive oil, dried fruits, nuts,

pine kernels, innumerable aromatic plants and spice mixtures played a great part in this cuisine as did 'garum', which today is never seen in Italy.

After the fall of the Roman empire, Italy was split up and the resultant mosaic of independent states was, curiously enough, the catalyst for an extraordinary culinary renaissance. New produce arrived from everywhere, including sugar, maize, haricot beans and, importantly, pasta, and was immediately adopted throughout the country. And lastly the tomato made its appearance and with it came a revolution. Prior to this Neapolitan sauce had been made with onions – the sauce known today as Genoese sauce!

A country of many states until 1861, Italy was proud of its regional specialities and even after unification continued to cultivate the gastronomic differences of its 18 provinces and many large and small towns, which love and produce good cooking. *Bollito misto, vitello tonnato, polenta* and *zabaglione* still all come from Turin; *pesto* dishes from Genoa; *risotto giallo*, *osso bucco* and *panettone* from Milan; *risotto nero* and *carpaccio* from Venice; *salsa verde* and *salsa bolognese* from Bologna; aubergines *au gratin* and baked lasagnes from Parma; *cacciucco*, *fagioli al fiasco* and *zuccotto* from Tuscany; *panforte*, stuffed artichokes, *saltimbocca* and *torta di ricotta* from Rome; *spaghetti aiglo e oglio*, *salsa al pomodoro*, *pizza*, rice cake – once made of German wheat – from Naples; *caponata*, *pasta alla Norma* and water-melon ice from Sicily; *culingioni* – meatless pasta – and *sebada* – white cheese and honey cakes – from Sardinia.

Italian cookery has a hundred different sides to it. The Italians produce thousands of wonderful things like *parmigiano reggiano*, *mozzarella* (made from ox milk), the sweetest olive oil in the world and rice from the valley of the Po and they have magnificent vineyards from the north to the south of the country. And there are probably hundreds of still unknown recipes simmering away on the cookers of Italian mammas!

# GNOCCHI ALLA ROMANA

## *Gnocchi Roman-style*

Also known in Rome as 'semolina gnocchi' or 'gnocchi di semmolella'.

SERVES 4

*1 litre/1¾ pints milk*
*150 g/5 oz butter*
*150 g/5 oz semolina*
*2 egg yolks*
*75 g/3 oz fresh parmesan, grated finely*
*salt*

1 Pour the milk into a large saucepan. Add 50 g/2 oz of the butter and some salt and bring the milk to the boil.

2 Pour the semolina in a stream into the boiling milk and stir well for about 15 minutes, until it pulls away from the sides of the saucepan. Remove the saucepan from the heat and mix in the egg yolks and 1 tablespoon of the grated parmesan, stirring continuously.

3 Lightly butter a large baking tray. Turn the gnocchi mixture into this and smooth the surface with a pliable spatula; it should be no more than 1 cm/½ inch thick. Leave it to go cold.

4 Preheat the oven to Gas Mark 7/220°C/425°F. Melt the remaining butter in a small saucepan. When the gnocchi mixture is really cold, cut it into 5 cm/2-inch rounds using a plain biscuit cutter (2-inch diameter).

5 Brush the melted butter around the inside of an oval 30 cm/12-inch gratin dish and arrange the gnocchi on this in 4 layers, one on top of the other, piling them up into a dome shape. Coat each layer with melted butter and grated parmesan as you go along.

6 Transfer the dish to the oven and cook the gnocchi for 25 minutes, just until they turn golden. Serve them hot from the gratin dish.

# MACARONI ALL'AMATRICIANA

## *Macaroni Amatrice-style*

This is the original recipe for pasta *all'amatriciana*, that is to say from the little town of Amatrice in the Abbruzzi.

SERVES 4

*200 g/7 oz pancetta (Italian bacon)*
*1 tablespoon olive oil*
*1 small dried chilli*
*375 g/12 oz fine macaroni*
*100 g/3½ oz fresh Pecorino cheese, grated finely*
*salt and pepper*

1 Cut the pancetta into small strips and put them into a saucepan. Add the olive oil, crumble in the chilli and put the pan on a low heat. Cook the pancetta for 5-7 minutes, until it lightly browns.

2 Cook the pasta in a large pan of boiling salted water and when it is cooked *al dente*, drain it and turn it out into a deep dish. Add the pancetta and half the Pecorino, add pepper and mix well. Serve immediately, with the rest of the Pecorino offered separately.

# SALTIMBOCCA ALLA ROMANA

## *Saltimbocca Roman-style*

SERVES 2

*2 thin slices veal fillet*
*2 thin slices Parma ham, cut from the widest part of the ham*
*8 sage leaves*
*1 tablespoon olive oil*
*20 g/¾ oz butter*
*3 tablespoons dry white wine*
*salt and pepper*

**1** Ask the butcher to beat out the veal slices as thinly as possible. Cut each slice of Parma ham into quarters and place one on top of each piece of veal. Decorate each slice with a sage leaf and pin them flat with wooden toothpicks.

**2** Heat the olive oil in a large frying pan. Add the butter, and when it has melted, brown the saltimbocca over a low heat for 1 minute on the veal side and 5 seconds on the ham side. Arrange the saltimbocca on two dishes and set them aside, keeping them warm.

**3** Pour the wine into the pan and deglaze the cooking juices, stirring well with a wooden spatula. Cook the sauce until it has reduced by half, season it and coat the saltimbocca with it. Serve immediately, accompanied by polenta (page 37) or fresh buttered pasta.

# POLLO ALLA ROMANA

## *Chicken with Peppers Roman-style*

SERVES 6

*1 chicken, 1.75 kg/4 lb, cut into 12 pieces*
*6 large fresh garlic cloves*
*2 tablespoons olive oil*
*3 sprigs fresh thyme, chopped finely*
*3 sprigs fresh rosemary, chopped finely*
*400 g/13 oz just ripe tomatoes*
*2 large red peppers*
*salt and pepper*

**1** Skin the chicken pieces and make small deep cuts in the meat, through to the bone. Cut the garlic cloves in half.

**2** Put the chicken pieces into a shallow dish, sprinkle them with 1 tablespoon of the oil and stir so that each piece is uniformly coated. Add the garlic, thyme, rosemary, salt and pepper and mix well again. Leave to marinate for 30 minutes.

**3** Meanwhile, scald the tomatoes in boiling water for 10 seconds, cool them under cold running water, skin, halve and de-seed them. Roughly chop the flesh. Wash the peppers, cut them into quarters vertically and remove the stalk, seeds and white pith. Cut them into 2 x 3 cm/1 x 1½-inch strips.

**4** Heat the remaining oil in a large casserole. Add the marinated chicken and strips of pepper. Cover the casserole and leave to cook for 40 minutes, on a low heat, turning the pieces every 5 minutes using two wooden spatulas.

**5** At the end of this time, add the tomato. Stir well, cover the casserole with a lid and leave to cook for 10 minutes, turning once or twice. Turn out into a deep serving dish and serve hot, warm or cold.

# OSSOBUCO ALLA MILANESE

## *Knuckle of Veal Milanese-style*

SERVES 4

*4 pieces veal knuckle, 3 cm/1¼ inch thick (about 1.5 kg/3½ lb)*
*1 small onion*
*1 garlic clove*
*40 g/1½ oz butter*
*125 ml/4 fl oz dry white wine*
*300 ml/½ pint water*
*grated zest of 1 small lemon*
*salt and pepper*

**1** Wash and wipe dry the meat. Chop the onion finely and cut the garlic clove in half.

**2** Melt the butter in a buffet casserole and brown the veal knuckle in this for 6-7 minutes on each side, seasoning as you turn them. Add the onion and half the crushed garlic. Stir for 1 minute, then pour in the wine and leave it to cook until the liquid has evaporated. Then add 100 ml/3½ fl oz of the water and cook until the water is also absorbed. Add a further 100 ml/3½ fl oz of the water, bring it to the boil, put the lid on and leave the meat to cook over a low heat for 2 hours, checking it and adding a little more water regularly (a total of 300 ml/½ pint should suffice) so that the meat is always cooking in the rich, thick gravy. Turn the meat several times during cooking.

**3** At the end of 2 hours, add 3-4 tablespoons of water to deglaze and produce a syrupy gravy of coating consistency. Add the remaining crushed garlic and the zest of lemon. Turn the meat in this fragrant sauce, cook for a further 2 minutes and serve with fresh buttered pasta and grated parmesan cheese or with risotto alla milanese (page 35).

# Fegato alla Veneziana
## Calves' Liver Venetian-style

### SERVES 4

*500 g/1 lb mild onions, e.g. Spanish*
*4 tablespoons olive oil*
*25 g/1 oz butter*
*3 tablespoons chopped flat-leaf parsley*
*625 g/1¼ lb calves' liver, cut into 2 slices*
*1 tablespoon dry white vermouth*
*salt and pepper*

**1** Chop the onions finely.

**2** Put the olive oil into a small buffet casserole on a low heat and add the butter. When this has melted, add the onions, parsley, salt and pepper. Stir for 2 minutes, then cover the pan and leave the onions to cook for 45 minutes on a low heat, turning from time to time.

**3** Meanwhile, wash the slices of liver and wipe them dry. Slice them diagonally into 1 cm/½-inch thick strips.

**4** At the end of the onions' cooking time, add the liver to the pan and cook it on a higher heat, stirring continuously, until it is done. Add the vermouth and the equivalent amount of water and stir well for 30 seconds.

**5** Divide the liver and onions among 4 warmed plates. Serve immediately with polenta (page 37).

# Peposo
## Beef Stew with Pepper

During the construction of the dome of the church of Santa Maria del Fiore in Florence, the tile-makers, who came from Impruneta, would warm up their peposo in small earthenware cocottes in their kiln. It is said that Filippo Brunelleschi, the fifteenth-century Italian Renaissance sculptor and architect, was very fond of it.

### SERVES 6

*1.5 kg/3½ lb shin of beef*
*750 g/1½ lb just ripe tomatoes*
*12 garlic cloves*
*1 tablespoon finely ground black pepper*
*1 teaspoon fine rock salt*
*200 ml/7 fl oz water*
*2 pinches sugar*
*300 ml/½ pint Italian red wine, e.g. Chianti, Barbera d'Asti*

**1** Cut the meat into 2 cm/¾-inch cubes. Wash the tomatoes, halve them and put them through a blender or food processor until they are coarsely chopped. Cut the garlic cloves into slivers, discarding the sprouting part if the garlic is old.

**2** Put the meat into a large cocotte. Add the tomatoes, garlic, pepper, salt, water and sugar. Stir well and cover the cocotte with a lid.

**3** Set the oven at Gas Mark ½/130°C/250°F. Transfer the cocotte to the oven and leave the meat and tomatoes to cook without disturbing for 2½ hours.

**4** At the end of this time, stir in the wine and leave the stew to cook for a further 2½ hours.

**5** At the end of 5 hours' cooking the meat will have turned into a delicious, fragrant stew. Serve immediately in the cocotte, accompanied by polenta (page 37) or fresh pasta.

## ITALY

Polenta

Peposo
*(Beef Stew with Pepper)*

Macaroni all'Amatriciana
*(Macaroni Amatrice-style)*

# INVOLTINI ALLA TOSCANA

## *Veal Olives Tuscan-style*

SERVES 4

*8 very thin veal escalopes, cut from the eye of the
fillet
200 g/7 oz Parma ham
8 sage leaves
400 g/13 oz ripe tomatoes
100 g/3½ oz carrots
2 celery sticks, tender inner ones
150 g/5 oz onions
3 tablespoons olive oil
20 g/¾ oz butter
100 ml/3½ fl oz dry white wine
salt and pepper*

**1** Ask the butcher to beat out the escalopes as
thinly as possible. Roughly chop the ham and
spread it over each escalope to within 1 cm/½ inch
of the edges. Place a sage leaf in the centre of each.
Roll the meat up on itself, starting with the smallest
side. Tie up the resultant little parcel with kitchen
string. Prepare all 8 escalopes in the same way.

**2** Scald the tomatoes in boiling water for 10 seconds, cool them under cold running water, skin,
halve and de-seed them; roughly chop the flesh.
Peel the carrots and chop them finely together with
the celery and onions.

**3** Heat the olive oil in a large casserole. Brown the
veal olives all over, turning them 2 or 3 times using
two wooden spatulas. Remove them from the pan
and set them aside on a large plate.

**4** Add the butter to the casserole and, when it has
melted, the finely chopped vegetables. Stir well.
Cover the casserole and leave the vegetables to
simmer over a very low heat for 10 minutes until
they are tender. Put the veal olives back into the
casserole and pour the wine over them. Leave to
cook until the wine has completely evaporated,
then add the tomato. Season and stir well. Cover
the casserole with a lid and leave the veal to cook for
a further 1½ hours on a low heat, stirring from time
to time.

**5** At the end of this time, take the veal olives out
and set them aside to keep hot. Leave the sauce to
reduce over a moderate heat.

**6** While the sauce is reducing, remove the string
from the veal olives, placing them in a warm serving
dish as you finish each one. Coat them with the
sauce and serve them immediately with creamed
potatoes or haricot beans in olive oil (page 36).

# CONIGLIO IN UMIDO

## *Rabbit in White Wine and Tomato*

SERVES 4

*1 rabbit, 1.5 kg/3½ lb
250 g/8 oz ripe tomatoes
2 tablespoons olive oil
20 g/¾ oz butter
2 bay leaves
1 sprig rosemary
2 sage leaves
2 garlic cloves
100 ml/3½ fl oz dry white wine
2 tablespoons pine kernels
4 pinches grated nutmeg
salt and pepper*

**1** Ask the butcher to cut the rabbit into 8 pieces.
Wash the meat and wipe dry. Season it. Scald the
tomatoes in boiling water for 10 seconds, cool
them under cold running water, skin, halve and de-
seed them. Roughly chop the flesh.

**2** Heat the olive oil in a buffet casserole. Add the
butter and when it has melted, brown the rabbit
pieces in it with the bay leaves, rosemary, sage and
whole garlic cloves. Drain off the cooking fat and
pour in the wine. Stir until the wine has completely
evaporated and the rabbit pieces are well browned.
Add the pine kernels, nutmeg and tomato. Stir,
cover the casserole, and leave the rabbit to cook for
1 hour, stirring from time to time.

**3** When the rabbit is cooked, serve immediately
from the dish, accompanied by fresh pasta or
polenta (page 37).

# TRIGLIE ALLA LIVORNESE

## *Grey Mullet Livorno-style*

SERVES 4

*500 g/1 lb ripe tomatoes*
*3 garlic cloves*
*1 celery stick, a tender inner one, with leaves*
*6 tablespoons olive oil*
*3 tablespoons chopped flat-leaf parsley*
*8 medium mullet (about 200 g/7 oz each)*
*3 tablespoons flour*
*salt and pepper*

1 First make the tomato sauce. Scald the tomatoes for 10 seconds in boiling water, cool them under cold running water, skin, halve and de-seed them; finely chop the flesh. Chop the garlic finely. Wash the celery, wipe it dry and chop it into small pieces.

2 Heat 2 tablespoons of the olive oil in a medium saucepan. Put in half the parsley, the garlic and the celery. Stir for 1 minute over a very low heat, then add the tomato. Season the sauce and leave it to cook for 15 minutes on a moderate heat, stirring often. Give quick stirs to the sauce; it should not be too smooth.

3 Ask the fishmonger to clean the mullet, leaving the strongly scented and iodised livers inside them. Wash them and wipe dry. Roll them in the flour and shake them to remove any excess.

4 Heat the rest of the oil in a large frying pan. Fry the fish a few at a time in this until golden – 3 minutes each side, seasoning during cooking. Then set them aside in a dish to keep warm.

5 Pour the tomato sauce into the pan and heat it through in the strongly flavoured cooking juices from the fish. When it's really hot, coat the mullet with the sauce and serve immediately, with haricot beans in olive oil (page 36).

# ALICI IN TORTIERA

## *Anchovies Gratinéed*

SERVES 4

*750 g/1½ lb fresh anchovies*
*2 garlic cloves*
*75 g/3 oz stale white bread*
*3 tablespoons chopped flat-leaf parsley*
*4 tablespoons olive oil*
*salt and pepper*

1 Preheat the oven to Gas Mark 7/220°C/425°F. Lightly oil a baking dish large enough to hold all the anchovies in two layers.

2 Gut and head the fish. Wash them and wipe dry. Mince the garlic finely. Make the bread into large breadcrumbs using a food processor or the coarse side of a grater. Mix the breadcrumbs, parsley and garlic together.

3 Arrange a layer of anchovies in the baking dish and spread half the breadcrumb mixture over them. Sprinkle half the olive oil over that and season. Place the second layer of anchovies on top of the first and spread over the remaining breadcrumbs. Sprinkle with the remaining oil and season.

4 Transfer the dish to the oven and leave the anchovies to cook for 20 minutes until they are browned on top. Serve them hot straight from the baking dish.

# SARDELLE IN SAOR

## *Sweet and Sour Sardines*

In Venice, small sole are cooked in the same way.

SERVES 6

*50 g/2 oz small white seedless grapes*
*625 g/1¼ lb mild onions*
*200 ml/7 fl oz groundnut oil*
*1 level tablespoon caster sugar*
*50 g/2 oz pine kernels*
*4 pinches ground cinnamon*
*150 ml/¼ pint dry white wine*
*300 ml/½ pint white wine vinegar*
*2 pinches ground cloves*
*1 kg/2 lb fresh sardines, 25–35 g/1–1¼ oz each,*
*cleaned*
*4 tablespoons flour*
*salt and pepper*

**1** Rinse the grapes and soak them in warm water. Mince the onions.

**2** Heat 4 tablespoons of the groundnut oil in a large saucepan. Put in the onions and cook them on a low heat for about 20 minutes until they turn golden, turning them frequently. Add the sugar and leave the onions to caramelise lightly. Add the drained grapes, pine kernels, cinnamon, wine, vinegar, salt, pepper and ground cloves. Bring the liquid to the boil, and leave it to boil up for 5 minutes before taking the pan off the heat and covering it with a lid.

**3** Wash and dry the cleaned sardines. Roll them quickly in the flour, dusting off any excess.

**4** Heat the remaining oil in a large frying pan; the oil should be 1 cm/½ inch deep; if it's not, add more. Quickly brown both sides of the sardines in this, then drain them on kitchen paper.

**5** Heat the contents of the saucepan through and spread an even layer of the sweet and sour onion mixture on the bottom of a 22 cm/8½-inch round gratin dish. Arrange the sardines in a head to tail pattern in the dish and coat them with the remaining sweet and sour mixture. Cover the dish and leave the sardines to marinate, refrigerated, for 24 hours before serving at room temperature.

# SPAGHETTI ALLA NAPOLETANA

## *Spaghetti Neapolitan-style*

SERVES 4

*500 g/1 lb ripe tomatoes*
*1 garlic clove*
*2 tablespoons olive oil*
*4 pinches dried oregano*
*375 g/12 oz fine spaghetti*
*2 tablespoons finely chopped basil*
*salt and pepper*
*fresh parmesan, grated finely, to serve*

**1** Scald the tomatoes for 10 seconds in boiling water, cool them under cold running water, skin, halve and de-seed them; chop the flesh finely. Chop the garlic clove finely.

**2** Heat the olive oil in a large saucepan. Put in the garlic and cook it over a low heat until it turns golden. Then add the tomato, oregano, salt and pepper. Stir well and leave the sauce to cook for 20 minutes on a moderate heat, stirring from time to time.

**3** When the tomato sauce is ready, cook the pasta in a large pan of salted boiling water and, when it is cooked *al dente*, drain it in a colander. Turn it into a deep dish and coat with the sauce. Sprinkle the spaghetti and sauce with basil and serve it immediately with grated parmesan on the side.

# MINESTRONE TOSCANO

## *Tuscan-style Minestrone*

SERVES 4–5

*100 g/3½ oz dried cannellini beans, soaked for 8
hours
4 ripe tomatoes
1 small Savoy cabbage
2 carrots
1 small onion
1 garlic clove
1 small bunch flat-leaf parsley
1 celery stick
50 g/2 oz lean bacon, preferably Italian pancetta
6 tablespoons olive oil
6 single sprigs rosemary
1 sprig thyme
150 g/5 oz cut macaroni, large pasta shells or ditali
salt and pepper*

**1** Drain the beans, put them in a large saucepan
and cover them generously with cold water. Bring
them to the boil and leave to cook for 1 hour over
a low heat: the beans should be very tender.

**2** Meanwhile, scald the tomatoes in boiling water
for 10 seconds, cool them under cold running
water, skin, halve and de-seed them; roughly chop
the flesh. Slice the cabbage very finely. Peel and
wash the carrots. Chop the carrots, onion, garlic,
parsley leaves, celery and bacon and turn them into
a large casserole with the olive oil. Stir for 2-3
minutes over a low heat until the vegetables have
softened.

**3** As soon as the beans are cooked, drain them,
reserving the cooking liquid. Put half the beans
through a food processor or sieve them. Put the
whole beans, bean purée and cooking liquid into
the casserole with the tomatoes, rosemary, thyme
and cabbage. Completely cover them with water,
season the soup, cover the casserole and leave to
cook for 1 hour on a low heat.

**4** At the end of this time, add the pasta, stir, and
leave the soup to simmer for a further 30 minutes.

**5** This thick, fragrant soup should not be served
too hot, and it doesn't need grated cheese. If
desired, 6 snipped leaves of basil may be added at
the same time as the vegetables.

# RISOTTO ALLA MILANESE

## *Risotto Milanese-style*

SERVES 4

*40 g/1½ oz beef marrow
1.25 litres/2¼ pints very hot chicken or beef stock
2 pinches saffron strands
75 g/3 oz butter
1 small onion
300 g/10 oz risotto rice
100 ml/3½ fl oz dry white wine
50 g/2 oz fresh parmesan cheese, grated finely*

**1** The night before, put the beef marrow into a
bowl and cover it with salted water. Leave it in the
refrigerator for 12 hours.

**2** The next day, put 100 ml/3½ fl oz of the stock
into a small saucepan and bring it to the boil. Add
the saffron, remove the pan from the heat and leave
it to infuse until the stock is needed. Wash the beef
marrow well, wipe it and cut it into small cubes.
Turn it into a separate small saucepan with half the
butter. Chop the onion finely and add it to the pan.
Leave the marrow to cook over a low heat for 10
minutes until it melts.

**3** Strain the contents of the pan into a large casserole. Place the casserole on a medium heat and pour
the rice in all at once on top of the hot marrowy
liquid. Cook the rice for 5 minutes, stirring continuously; it should turn pale yellow. Moisten the
rice with the white wine and as soon as this is
absorbed, add the stock in 5 or 6 lots, still stirring
continuously, allowing the rice to absorb each lot
of stock before adding the next. Finish with the
saffron stock, strained to remove the pieces of
saffron.

**4** Allow about 20 minutes for the rice to absorb all
the stock and stir frequently throughout this time.
Finally, add the remaining butter, stirring well,
then the parmesan, turning and folding it in for 30
seconds. Remove the casserole from the heat,
cover it and leave the risotto to rest for 2 minutes.
Bring it to the table in its casserole.

# FAGIOLI STUFATI

## *Haricot Beans in Olive Oil*

In Tuscany the beans are cooked *al fiasco*, literally in the flask: they are put into a Chianti bottle (which has been thoroughly cleaned and the label and cork removed) with water, oil, sage and garlic. A 'cork' of cotton wool is placed in the top, so some of the vapour can escape. Three hours of cooking over a very, very low heat immersed in hot water and the beans are done, really soft and imbued with olive oil. They are as delicious hot as cold.

SERVES 4

*400 g/13 oz dried haricot beans, boiled 10 minutes*
*2 sage leaves*
*4 tablespoons olive oil*
*1 teaspoon lemon juice*
*salt and pepper*

**1** Put the beans into a large casserole. Add 2 litres water and the sage leaves. Cover the casserole, and leave the beans to simmer over a very, very low heat for 4 hours; the water must never boil. Do not stir the beans during cooking.

**2** At the end of this time, the beans are cooked and soft. Add the olive oil and lemon juice and season. Stir the beans carefully and serve them immediately.

# CARCIOFI CON PATATE IN UMIDO

## *Artichokes with Potato*

These vegetables make an excellent accompaniment to lamb, goat, poultry and roasted white meats.

SERVES 4

*6 potatoes, 100 g/3½ oz each, firm variety*
*6 globe artichokes, 200 g/7 oz each*
*½ a lemon*
*1 garlic clove*
*3 tablespoons olive oil*
*1 tablespoon chopped flat-leaf parsley*
*salt and pepper*

**1** Peel, wash, quarter and dry the potatoes in a tea towel. Cut the artichoke stalks off 15 mm/ ⅝ inch below the heart. Break off all the tough outer leaves, leaving the inner leaves intact. Cut the tender leaves 1 cm/½ inch from the heart. Peel and trim the hearts, cut them in quarters, remove the hairy choke and rub them with the lemon half. Chop the garlic finely.

**2** Put 3 tablespoons of water into a medium casserole. Bring it to the boil and add the olive oil. As soon as the mixture has emulsified, drop in the potatoes and the rinsed and drained artichokes. Add the garlic and parsley. Season with salt. Cover the casserole with a lid and leave the vegetables to cook for 15 minutes on a medium heat, stirring two or three times.

**3** At the end of this time, the artichokes and potatoes will be tender and the water will have evaporated. Season with pepper and serve immediately.

# BIETE AL POMODORO

## *Swiss Chard with Tomato*

These vegetables go well with fried fish and grilled or roasted white meats.

SERVES 3–4

*625 g/1¼ lb sticks of young Swiss chard*
*250 g/8 oz ripe, but firm tomatoes*
*6 anchovy fillets in oil*
*2 garlic cloves*
*1 small fresh chilli*
*2 tablespoons olive oil*
*pepper*

**1** Wash the sticks of chard and cut them into 1 x 5 cm/½ x 2-inch diagonal strips, carefully removing the stringy pith. Rinse the chard but don't dry it completely. Scald the tomatoes in boiling water for 10 seconds, cool them under cold running water, skin, halve and de-seed them; roughly chop the flesh. Dice the anchovies. Cut the garlic cloves in half, discarding the sprouting part if necessary. Wash the chilli, chop it finely and de-seed.

**2** Heat the olive oil in a large casserole. Add the chilli and garlic. When the garlic has just started to go brown, remove it from the casserole and put in the tomato. Stir for 5 minutes before adding the chard. Stir well and leave the chard to cook on a low heat for about 20 minutes with the lid on.

**3** At the end of this time, remove the lid: the chard should be tender and all the water should have evaporated. Add the anchovy fillets. Leave to simmer, uncovered, on a very low heat for 3 minutes, the length of time it takes to melt the anchovies; then remove the casserole from the heat. Add pepper to taste just before serving.

# POLENTA
## *Polenta*

Polenta is made all over Italy; it is 'yellow' in the north because it is made with maize, and 'white' in the south because it is made with wheat. The capital, Rome, forms the border between the two regions.

This dish may also be prepared in advance, sprinkled with cheese, put in the oven and served *au gratin*. Once cooled, polenta may be sliced, put in the oven to brown, or sautéd in a pan, thus transforming it into crunchy biscuits.

### SERVES 6

*50 g/2 oz butter*
*250 g/8 oz semolina, finely ground*
*salt and pepper*

**1** Pour 1 litre/1¾ pints of water into a large saucepan, add the butter and bring it to the boil. Season well and lower the heat.

**2** Pour the semolina in a stream into the boiling water, stirring continuously with a wooden spatula. Cook, still stirring continuously, until the mixture is smooth and forms a compact whole, pulling away from the sides of the saucepan. The cooking time varies according to the type of semolina used – 15–20 minutes on average, with 3–5 minutes for precooked semolina.

**3** Take the pan off the heat. Turn the polenta out into a shallow dish and spread it evenly in a 4–5 cm/ 1½–2 inch layer, using a spatula. Serve immediately, cutting it into slices at the table.

# MELANZANE ALLA PARMIGIANA
## *Aubergines with Parmesan Cheese*

### SERVES 4–6

*1 kg/2 lb aubergines*
*1 tablespoon cooking salt*
*200 ml/7 fl oz olive oil*
*200 ml/7 fl oz groundnut oil*
*350 g/12 oz mozzarella cheese*
*100 g/3½ oz fresh parmesan cheese, grated finely*
*500 g/1 lb fresh, plain tomato sauce (see Spaghetti alla Napoletana, page 34)*
*24 small basil leaves*
*salt*

**1** Wash the aubergines and cut them into 1 cm/½-inch slices, lengthwise. Sprinkle them with the cooking salt and leave them to drain for an hour, upright in a colander. Wash them thoroughly and wipe them dry with kitchen paper.

**2** Put the two oils into a large frying pan to a depth of 1 cm/½ inch. Fry the aubergine slices in this, on both sides, then drain them well on kitchen paper. Add more oil as necessary during cooking.

**3** Preheat the oven to Gas Mark 4/180°C/350°F. Cut the mozzarella into 5 mm/¼-inch cubes. Arrange one-third of the aubergines in a 30 cm/12-inch oven dish in rows. Cover with one-third of the parmesan, one-third of the mozzarella and one-third of the tomato sauce. Continue in the same way with 2 more layers. Sprinkle each layer, except the last, with basil leaves. Transfer the dish to the oven and cook the aubergines for 30 minutes.

**4** Serve hot, warm or cool.

# ITALY

Melanzane alla Parmigiana
*(Aubergines with Parmesan Cheese)*

Fagioli Stufati
*(Haricot Beans in Olive Oil)*

Biete al Pomodoro
*(Swiss Chard with Tomato)*

# TIRAMISÙ

This delicious speciality of Verona is made with mascarpone, a very creamy soft white cheese, which can now be bought here. Amaretto is a liqueur with a delicate almond flavour.

SERVES 6

For the biscuit pastry base:
*6 eggs*
*150 g/5 oz caster sugar*
*150 g/5 oz plain flour*
*1 teaspoon vanilla essence*
*1 pinch salt*

For the topping:
*4 eggs*
*200 g/7 oz caster sugar*
*500 g/1 lb mascarpone cheese*
*500 ml/18 fl oz strong coffee*
*100 ml/3½ fl oz amaretto liqueur*

To serve:
*bitter cocoa powder*

1 First make the biscuit pastry base. Preheat the oven to Gas Mark 6/200°C/400°F. Separate the eggs. Reserve the whites in a large bowl and sprinkle them with salt. Put the yolks into a mixing bowl and add the sugar. Whisk until the mixture turns white, then sieve in the flour, fold it in with a spatula and mix in the vanilla.

2 Beat the egg whites to a firm snow and carefully fold them into the flour and yolk mixture, using a spatula.

3 Butter a 28 x 38 cm/11 x 15-inch non-stick baking tray and line it with greaseproof paper. Turn the biscuit pastry mixture out on to this, smoothing the top with a spatula. Transfer the baking tray to the oven and cook the biscuit pastry for 7–8 minutes until it turns golden.

4 Take the baking tray out of the oven. Spread a damp tea towel on a work surface and turn the biscuit pastry base out on to this. Remove the greaseproof paper and leave it to cool.

5 Next, prepare the topping. Separate the eggs. Set aside the whites in a large bowl. Put the yolks into a mixing bowl and add the sugar. Whisk this

until the mixture turns white, then add the mascarpone cheese, still whisking.

6 Beat the egg whites to a firm snow and carefully fold them into the previous mixture, using a spatula.

7 Finally, assemble the tiramisù. Cut the biscuit pastry into two 14 x 19 cm/5½ x 7½-inch rectangles. Pour the coffee into a bowl and add the liqueur. Put one half of the biscuit pastry into a rectangular flan dish just large enough to hold it and sprinkle it with the coffee and liqueur mixture. Spread half the mascarpone cream topping over it. Place the second piece of biscuit pastry on top and moisten it with the remaining coffee/liqueur mixture. Top that with the remaining mascarpone cream topping and put the tiramisù into the refrigerator. Leave it to chill for at least 2 hours.

8 When you are ready to serve it, take the tiramisù out of the refrigerator, dust it with cocoa powder, using a sieve, and serve immediately.

# TORTA DI RICOTTA

## *Ricotta Gâteau*

SERVES 6

*5 eggs*
*500 g/1 lb Italian ricotta (pure ewe's milk cheese)*
*1 heaped tablespoon flour*
*100 g/3½ oz caster sugar*
*zest of 1 unwaxed lemon*
*2 tablespoons candied orange or citron peel, chopped finely*
*½ teaspoon ground cinnamon*
*2 tablespoons dark rum*

1 Preheat the oven to Gas Mark 2/150°C/300°F. Butter a 24 cm/9½-inch deep cake tin. Separate the whites and yolks of 4 eggs, keeping the yolks in their shells and putting the whites into a large bowl.

2 Grate the ricotta over a bowl, through the fine side of a grater. Add the egg yolks and the remaining whole egg and mix well. Sieve in the flour, all but 2 tablespoons of the sugar, the zest of lemon, the fruit peel, 2 pinches of the cinnamon and the rum. Mix them all together well.

3 Beat the egg whites to a firm snow and fold them

into the ricotta mixture. Turn the mixture into the buttered cake tin and transfer it to the oven. Leave the gâteau to cook for 45 minutes, then remove it from the heat and leave it to stand for 15 minutes before turning it out on to a serving dish. Dust the top with the remaining caster sugar and cinnamon mixed together, and serve it hot, warm or cold.

# DOLCE DI CASTAGNE

## *Chestnut Dessert*

SERVES 6

*5 eggs*
*150 g/5 oz sugar*
*50 g/2 oz ground almonds*
*½ teaspoon vanilla essence*
*500 g/1 lb plain chestnut purée*

For the cake tin:
*1 knob butter*
*15 g/½ oz sugar*

**1** Preheat the oven to Gas Mark 2/150°C/300°F. Butter a non-stick 24 cm/9½-inch cake tin. Sprinkle the base and sides with sugar, turning it from side to side so the sugar sticks to all inside surfaces.

**2** Separate the eggs. Set aside the whites in a large bowl and the yolks in a separate one. Add 100 g/3½ oz of the sugar to the yolks and whisk until the mixture doubles in volume. Now add the ground almonds and the vanilla. Whisk for 1 minute longer, then add the chestnut purée.

**3** Beat the egg whites to a firm snow, then add the remaining sugar, continuing to beat until they are smooth and glossy. Fold the chestnut mixture carefully in, using a spatula.

**4** Turn the mixture out into the cake tin and transfer it to the oven. Leave the dessert to cook for 45 minutes, then turn off the heat and leave it to stand for 5 minutes in the oven. Turn it out on to a serving dish and serve it at room temperature.

# TORTA DI RISO

## *Rice Pudding Italian-style*

SERVES 6

*1 litre/1¾ pints milk*
*250 g/8 oz short-grain rice*
*100 g/3½ oz sugar*
*100 g/3½ oz candied citron or assorted candied fruits*
*6 amaretti biscuits*
*5 eggs*
*100 g/3½ oz chopped almonds*
*finely grated zest of 1 lemon*

**1** Put the milk into a large saucepan and bring it to the boil. Rinse and drain the rice. Add it to the boiling milk and leave it to cook for 20–25 minutes, stirring often, until it is really soft. Remove the pan from the heat, add the sugar and stir until this has melted. Cover the pan and leave it to stand for 6–12 hours.

**2** Finely dice the candied citron or other candied fruit. Break up the amaretti into largish pieces.

**3** When the rice has stood long enough, preheat the oven to Gas Mark 4/180°C/350°F. Butter a 29 cm/11½-inch gratin dish.

**4** Beat the eggs well, then stir them into the rice and milk mixture. Add the citron, amaretti, almonds and zest of lemon. Mix well. Turn the mixture out into the dish and transfer it to the oven. Leave the pudding to cook for about 45 minutes, until the top turns a golden colour. Leave it to go cold and serve it straight from the cooking dish. This dessert is also delicious chilled.

# BELGIUM

## BELGIUM – A SMALL COUNTRY OF ONLY
*30,000 square kilometres – is made up of three areas: Flanders to the north,*

Wallonia to the south and Brussels in the centre. The Flemish people speak Flemish, the Walloons French and the people of Brussels both languages. Flanders, close to the Netherlands, is a marshy region; Wallonia is mountainous, wooded and threaded by waterways. It is bordered by the French part of Flanders, by Champagne and in the east, by Germany. The northern Belgians eat fish from the sea, crustaceans and shellfish, such dishes as *waterzooi*, marinated herrings, *moules marinières* with French fries, and prawn croquettes; in the south it is freshwater fish and game. But there are certain basic gastronomic delights which are common to all Belgian cuisine: the Belgian endives known as *chicons* or *witloof*, Brussels sprouts, raw, smoked Ardennes ham. There are, too, hundreds of local beers of the light Pils and Export type which are used for mutton stews, *moules marinières* or Flemish cod; the special brown ales, perfect for making *carbonades*; or the 'lambic' beers made with malted barley and wheat like '*kriek*' and '*gueuze*', in

which poultry and game, such as rabbit with prunes, may be simmered.

Traditional dishes smell of juniper, a favourite in Belgium, used to flavour *pékét*, a light alcohol made from grain which is served as a digestive and also with herrings, instead of beer.

The Belgians love sweet things, served of course at the end of a meal but also in the afternoon with coffee: they spread spiced bread with butter or chocolate spread or it can be eaten with raw ham or cooked cheese; waffles, coated with double cream or sprinkled with brown sugar; spicy biscuits like *speculoos*; sugar tarts – puff pastries covered in cream and caramelised brown sugar – with rice or custard cream; *tarte Liègeoise* with apples or plums; Brussels doughnuts with apple and cinnamon; the delicious, prettily presented chocolates called *pralines* and a thousand other treats of which each little village has its own specialities and which appear at *kermesse* time – the fêtes held in honour of the consecration of each village church.

# CREME BRUXELLOISE

## *Cream of Brussels Sprout Soup*

SERVES 6

*500 g/1 lb brussels sprouts, prepared*
*100 g/3½ oz onions*
*250 g/8 oz potatoes, floury variety*
*25 g/1 oz butter*
*150 g/5 oz piece of smoked bacon*
*600 ml/1 pint water*
*100 ml/3½ fl oz single cream*
*2 egg yolks*
*salt and pepper*

1 Rinse the brussels sprouts and wipe them dry. Mince the onions. Peel, wash and chop the potatoes into large cubes.

2 Melt the butter in a large round casserole. Add the onions and cook them for 5 minutes, stirring constantly, until they turn golden. Put in the bacon and brussels sprouts and stir them for 2 minutes. Add the water and the potatoes. Season with salt and pepper and, once the water has come up to the boil, cover the casserole with a lid, reduce the heat and leave to cook for 1 hour until the vegetables are thoroughly cooked through.

3 Remove the bacon with a slotted spoon and blend the contents of the pot to a very smooth cream. Pour it back into the pot and reheat it over a low heat.

4 Meanwhile, dice the bacon finely. Whisk the cream and egg yolks together with a fork and pour them into the hot soup, stirring continuously, but without allowing it to boil. Pour the soup into a warmed tureen and sprinkle it with the bacon. Serve it very hot, with slices of crispy toast.

# QUICHE FLAMANDE

## *Flemish Quiche*

SERVES 6

*750 g/1½ lb leeks, white and tender green parts only*
*50 g/2 oz butter*
*½ teaspoon caster sugar*
*4 pinches mixed spice*
*1 sprig thyme*
*250 ml/8 fl oz pale ale*
*300 g/10 oz flaky pastry*
*200 g/7 oz Parma ham, sliced finely*
*3 eggs*
*250 g/8 oz thick* crème fraîche *or 250 ml/8 fl oz double cream*
*salt and pepper*

1 Prepare the filling: wash and slice the leeks diagonally into 2 cm/¾-inch pieces. Melt the butter in a medium round casserole and put in the leeks, sugar, mixed spice, crushed thyme, salt and pepper. Stir until the leeks have turned golden. Add the beer, stir well and leave the filling to cook for 30 minutes, uncovered, stirring from time to time. Then remove the casserole from the heat.

2 Preheat the oven to Gas Mark 6/200°C/400°F. Roll out the pastry and line a 26 cm/10-inch flan dish with it. Cut the ham into 2 cm/¾-inch squares and pile them up on the pastry.

3 Beat the eggs with a fork, incorporating the cream, and salt and pepper. Pour this mixture over the still hot leeks and mix well. Turn the mixture out into the uncooked flan base and smooth the surface with a spatula.

4 Transfer the quiche to the oven and leave it to cook for about 30 minutes until golden in colour. Serve the quiche hot or warm.

## MOULES A L'OSTENDAISE

### *Mussels Ostend-style*

SERVES 4

*4 shallots*
*1 garlic clove*
*2 tablespoons chopped flat-leaf parsley*
*350 ml/12 fl oz dry white wine*
*3 kg/7 lb mussels*
*4 egg yolks*
*100 g/3½ oz thick* crème fraîche *or 250 ml/8 fl oz*
*double cream*
*3 tablespoons white breadcrumbs*

**1** Finely chop the shallots and garlic clove; put them into a very large round casserole, with the parsley and wine. Put the casserole on to a high heat and leave it to boil up for 5 minutes.

**2** Scrub the mussels and remove their beards. Discard any mussels that are cracked or shells that are open and do not close when sharply tapped. Wash them in several changes of water and add them to the pan. Leave them to open up over a high heat, then take them out with a slotted spoon and set them aside in a bowl. Discard any mussels that do not open after cooking.

**3** Strain the cooking juices and pour them into a small saucepan. Reduce the liquid by half over a high heat and then remove the pan from the heat. Whisk the egg yolks with the cream and stir this mixture into the contents of the saucepan, over a very low heat, not allowing it to boil, and keep stirring until the sauce is thick and smooth.

**4** Heat the grill. Remove the empty part of the shell from each mussel and arrange the open mussels on a 30 cm/12-inch baking dish. Coat them with the sauce and sprinkle them with breadcrumbs. Put the dish under the hot grill and leave the mussels to brown for 3 minutes. Serve them hot from the same dish.

## CABILLAUD A LA FLAMANDE

### *Cod Flemish-style*

SERVES 6

*1 x 1.25 kg/3 lb piece of cod (10 cm/4 inches in*
*diameter and 20 cm/8 inches long, cut from the*
*centre of a 3.5 kg/8 lb fish)*
*8 shallots*
*1 lemon*
*100 g/3½ oz butter*
*3 tablespoons chopped flat-leaf parsley*
*250 ml/8 fl oz dry white wine*
*salt and pepper*

**1** Preheat the oven to Gas Mark 7/220°C/425°F. Wash and wipe dry the fish. Season it with salt and pepper. Finely chop the shallots. Cut the lemon into very thin slices.

**2** Using 25 g/1 oz of the butter, grease a 30 cm/12-inch oven dish. Spread the shallots in this. Place the fish on top, stomach side down, and garnish it with the lemon slices. Sprinkle it with parsley, dot it with 25 g/1 oz of the butter and pour the wine over it. Transfer the dish to the oven and leave the fish to cook for 45 minutes.

**3** When the fish is cooked, set it aside to keep hot on a serving plate. Put the oven dish on a high heat on top of the cooker and reduce the cooking liquid until it is syrupy. Whisk in the remaining butter and take the dish off the heat.

**4** Skin the fish and take it off the bone. Divide the fillets between 6 warm plates. Coat them with the sauce and serve them with green vegetables and boiled potatoes.

# MOULES FARCIES AU VERT

## *Green Stuffed Mussels*

SERVES 6

*36 large mussels*
*1 kg/2 lb coarse rock salt*
*2 shallots*
*75 g/3 oz butter*
*50 g/2 oz fresh white bread*
*2 tablespoons chopped parsley*
*2 tablespoons chopped tarragon*
*pepper*

**1** Wash the mussels in several changes of water. Discard any mussels that are cracked or shells that are open and do not close when sharply tapped. Scrub them, remove their beards and put them into a very large round casserole with 3 tablespoons of water. Put the casserole on a high heat and leave the mussels to open up. Throw away any mussels that do not open. Reserve the cooking liquid. Cool the mussels slightly, then remove the empty half of the shells.

**2** Light the grill. Spread a 2 cm/¾-inch layer of rock salt in a flat oven dish, 30 cm/12 inches long. Arrange the mussels in their half shells on top, wedging them in well.

**3** Strain the mussel cooking liquid and put it into a small saucepan. Finely chop the shallots. Add them to the saucepan and bring to the boil. Leave the liquid to reduce by half, then add half the butter. Stir and remove the pan from the heat. Crumble in the bread, add the parsley and tarragon, season with pepper and stir well.

**4** Pile a little of this topping into each of the mussels and dot them with the remaining butter. Put the dish under the grill, not too close to the heat, and cook the mussels for 4–5 minutes until the topping turns golden.

**5** Serve the mussels hot from the cooking dish.

# WATERZOOI DE POISSONS

## *Poached Fish*

SERVES 6

*1.75 kg/4 lb mixed white fish, e.g. cod fillet, tail of monkfish, fillets of sole, etc., in large pieces*
*1 kg/2 lb mussels*
*4 celery sticks, tender inner ones with leaves*
*2 carrots*
*2 leeks, white parts only*
*75 g/3 oz butter*
*1.5 litres/2½ pints fish stock*
*100 g/3½ oz thick* crème fraîche *or 125 ml/4 oz double cream*
*1 tablespoon lemon juice*
*salt and pepper*

**1** Wash and wipe dry the fish. Scrub the mussels and remove their beards. Discard any mussels that are cracked or shells that are open and do not close when sharply tapped. Wash the mussels in several changes of water, then drain them and place them in a large round casserole with 125 ml/4 fl oz of water. Put the casserole on a high heat and leave the mussels to open, discarding any that fail to do so. Drain them and remove them from their shells. Strain the mussel liquid and set it aside with the mussels.

**2** Wash the celery. Peel the carrots and leeks and wash them. Chop all three vegetables finely.

**3** Melt the butter in the casserole and cook the vegetables in this until they turn golden. Lightly season them during cooking. Add the fish stock and mussel liquid to the pot, boil it up and then lower the heat before adding the white fish. Leave to simmer for 5 minutes, add the mussels to heat through and then remove the casserole from the heat.

**4** Using a slotted spoon, take out the fish and shellfish and arrange them in a tureen. Turn the heat up under the casserole and reduce the liquid for 5 minutes on a high heat. Add the cream and lemon juice, boil the liquid up again for a further 2 minutes, then remove from the heat. Pour the sauce over the fish in the tureen and serve immediately with slices of crisp toast and unsalted butter.

## BELGIUM

Quiche Flamande
*(Flemish Quiche)*

Gratin d'Endives au Jambon
*(Endive and Ham Gratin)*

Garniture Flamande
*(Flemish Vegetable Garnish)*

# HOCHEPOT

A Belgian version of the French _pot au feu_.

SERVES 8

_750 g/1½ lb stewing beef_
_500 g/1 lb breast of veal_
_500 g/1 lb neck of lamb_
_1 oxtail_
_300 g/10 oz smoked bacon, in a piece_
_1 large carrot_
_2 celery sticks, with their leaves_
_1 bouquet garni, consisting of 1 bay leaf, 1 sprig_
_thyme and 6 parsley stalks_
_1 onion_
_3 cloves_
_2 teaspoons coarse rock salt_
_1 teaspoon mixed pepper_
_2 garlic cloves_
_500 g/1 lb pork fillet_
_8 chipolata sausages_

For the vegetables:
_16 small carrots_
_16 small turnips_
_16 leeks, white parts only_
_2 celery hearts_
_16 small potatoes_
_salt_

**1** Prepare the meat: rinse it and wipe dry. Leave it in large pieces. Peel and wash the carrot with the celery sticks. Cut the carrot and celery into quarters. Tie up the ingredients for the bouquet garni. Stick the onion with the cloves.

**2** Put all the meat except the pork and sausages into a very large oval cocotte. Add the carrot, celery, onion, bouquet garni, salt, pepper and whole garlic cloves. Cover it all generously with cold water. Bring the broth to the boil, then leave it to simmer for 3 hours, skimming occasionally for the first half hour.

**3** Meanwhile, set the oven to Gas Mark 7/220°C/425°F. Put the pork fillet into an oven dish. Pop it into the hot oven and leave it to cook for 30 minutes, turning the meat several times, until it has browned on all sides. Fry the sausages in a dry pan until they are brown on all sides.

**4** Put the pork fillet into a saucepan, add a few spoonfuls of the broth from the meat; cover the pan and leave to cook gently for 1 hour. Add the sausages and cook both for a further 15 minutes. Turn off the heat, and keep the contents of the pan hot.

**5** When the meat in the cocotte is cooked, turn off the heat. Take out the onion, garlic and bouquet garni. Take the meat out of the broth and set both aside.

**6** Prepare the vegetables: peel the carrots, turnips and leeks. Wash these and the celery hearts and leave them whole. Put the vegetables into a large round casserole and add enough of the meat broth to half cover them. Cover the casserole and leave the vegetables to cook on a low heat until they are tender, about 20 minutes. Peel the potatoes, rinse them and put them in a saucepan. Cover them with water, bring it up to the boil, add salt and leave them to cook for about 20 minutes, until the potatoes are tender enough for the point of a knife to go in easily.

**7** Reheat the meat and the meat broth. Serve the broth in soup cups and the meat, bacon and sausages on a serving plate, sliced and surrounded by the vegetables.

# ASPERGES À LA FLAMANDE

## *Flemish-style Asparagus*

SERVES 4

*36 green asparagus spears*
*3 hard-boiled eggs*
*125 g/4 oz butter*
*1 tablespoon lemon juice*
*2 tablespoons snipped flat leaf parsley*
*salt and pepper*

**1** Wash and wipe dry the asparagus. Cut off the hard ends of the stalks and peel them. Sprinkle with salt and steam for 5–6 minutes until just tender.

**2** Shell and grate the eggs using the coarse side of a grater.

**3** Melt the butter in a large frying-pan. Put in the asparagus and fry for a few minutes until just golden, turning them over carefully. Season with salt and pepper.

**4** Using a draining spoon, divide the asparagus between 4 plates and sprinkle with grated egg. Put the lemon juice and parsley in the pan, stir once or twice and coat the asparagus with this butter, lemon and parsley sauce.

# SALADE LIÈGOISE

## *Liège-style Salad*

SERVES 6

*1 kg/ 2 lb firm potatoes*
*500 g/ 1 lb fine green beans*
*400 g/ 13 oz slightly salted bacon*
*1 onion*
*4 tablespoons groundnut oil*
*3 tablespoons wine vinegar*
*salt and pepper*

**1** Peel and slice the potatoes into 1 cm (½ inch) slices. Put into a saucepan and add cold water to cover. Bring to the boil, salt and leave to cook for about 15 minutes until tender.

**2** Top and tail, rinse, drain and cook the beans in salted boiling water for 5–7 minutes until just tender.

**3** Snip the bacon into thin strips and put into a medium frying-pan. Peel and finely chop the onion. Add to the pan with 1 tablespoon oil. Fry the bacon and onion, stirring continuously until just golden.

**4** When the potatoes and beans are cooked, drain and turn into a salad bowl.

**5** When the onion and bacon are soft and golden, drain and add to the salad. Pour the vinegar into the pan, bring to the boil, stirring and scraping with a spatula to deglaze the bacon cooking juices. Add the remaining oil and pour this hot vinaigrette sauce over the salad. Mix carefully and serve immediately.

# CARBONADES FLAMANDES

## *Flemish Carbonade of Beef*

SERVES 8

*1.75 kg/4 lb braising steak*
*300 g/10 oz onions*
*1 bouquet garni, consisting of 1 sprig thyme, 1 bay leaf and 6 parsley stalks*
*1 thick slice crusty white bread, about 75 g/3 oz*
*2 tablespoons English mustard*
*1 tablespoon oil*
*25 g/1 oz butter*
*1 tablespoon brown sugar*
*500 ml/18 fl oz beer (bitter)*
*salt and pepper*

**1** Cut the meat into 5 cm/2-inch cubes. Season it with salt and pepper. Finely chop the onions. Tie up the ingredients for the bouquet garni. Remove the crust from the bread and spread it with the mustard.

**2** Heat the oil in a large round casserole, and quickly seal the pieces of meat over a medium heat, cooking them for 2 minutes and stirring continuously. Set them aside on a dish. Melt the butter in the casserole and put in the onions. Stir well for 5 minutes until they turn golden. Add the brown sugar and leave the onions to caramelise lightly.

**3** Put the meat back into the casserole and mix it in with the onions. Add the bouquet garni and piece of bread. Pour on the beer: it should just cover the meat; if it doesn't, add a little more. Bring the liquid to the boil, cover the casserole and leave it to simmer for 4 hours on a very low heat without disturbing.

**4** At the end of this time, remove the meat from the casserole and keep it hot in a deep serving dish. Discard the bouquet garni. Put the gravy, bread and onion into a blender or food processor and blend until you have a smooth, oily consistency. Heat the sauce through on a low heat and pour it over the meat. Serve immediately.

# POULET A LA BIERE

## *Chicken in Beer*

SERVES 4–5

*1.75 kg/4 lb chicken, jointed into 10 pieces*
*150 g/5 oz smoked bacon*
*4 garlic cloves*
*100 g/3½ oz onions*
*2 tablespoons groundnut oil*
*25 g/1 oz butter*
*½ teaspoon caster sugar*
*350 ml/12 fl oz pale ale*
*salt and pepper*

**1** Rinse the chicken pieces and wipe them dry. Season them with salt and pepper. Cut the bacon into strips. Cut the garlic cloves in half. Finely chop the onions.

**2** Heat the oil in a large oval cocotte. Add the butter and, when it has melted, the chicken pieces. Brown them on all sides, then remove them from the cocotte and set them aside on a plate. Drain off the cooking fat and put the garlic, onions and bacon into the cocotte. Add the sugar and stir until everything turns golden.

**3** Put the chicken back into the cocotte and pour the beer over it. Stir well, bring it to the boil, then cover, reduce the heat and leave the chicken pieces to cook for 1–1¼ hours, turning them regularly.

**4** When the chicken is cooked, lift it out and keep it hot. Boil the sauce rapidly for several minutes to reduce and thicken it. Return the chicken to the cocotte and turn it in the sauce. Serve immediately with a Flemish vegetable garnish (page 51) or endives, either braised whole or sautéed in thin strips.

# MATOUFET

A Belgian speciality: not to be confused with the dessert version called 'matouflét', which of course does not use bacon but includes sugar and spices.

SERVES 4

*250 g/8 oz bacon, slightly salt*
*1 tablespoon groundnut oil*
*6 eggs*
*400 ml/14 fl oz milk*
*2 tablespoons flour*
*2 tablespoons chopped flat-leaf parsley*
*salt and pepper*

**1** Cut the bacon into fine slivers; blanch it for 1 minute in boiling water and drain. Heat the oil in a large frying pan and put in the bacon. Cook it until it starts to go brown, over a low heat, stirring continuously.

**2** Break the eggs into a bowl and beat them with a fork, incorporating the milk, flour, salt and pepper.

**3** Pour this mixture over the bacon and leave it to cook for 8–10 minutes over a low heat, stirring continuously until the mixture thickens. Add the parsley towards the end of cooking.

**4** Serve the matoufét hot, on thick slices of plain or toasted bread.

# GARNITURE FLAMANDE
## *Flemish Vegetable Garnish*

This garnish goes well with roast meat and poultry.

SERVES 4

*250 g/8 oz brussels sprouts*
*250 g/8 oz carrots*
*250 g/8 oz turnips*
*250 g/8 oz potatoes*
*1 garlic clove*
*100 g/3½ oz onions*
*100 g/3½ oz salted bacon*
*40 g/1½ oz butter*
*150 ml/¼ pint chicken stock*
*salt and pepper*

**1** Wash the brussels sprouts. Peel the carrots, turnips and potatoes. Rinse them and wipe dry. Cut the carrots in oval slices of 5 mm/¼ inch. Cut the potatoes in quarters lengthwise, then into fan shapes 5 mm/¼ inch thick. Cut the turnips into quarters.

**2** Cut the garlic clove into quarters. Chop the onions. Cut the bacon into strips and blanch it in boiling water for 1 minute. Drain and rinse it.

**3** Melt the butter in a large round casserole and put in the garlic, onion and strips of bacon. Stir until it all turns golden, then add the vegetables, and season. Pour on the stock, stir, cover the casserole and cook the garnish over a low heat for 30 minutes, stirring from time to time, until the vegetables are tender. Serve hot.

# ROGNONS DE VEAU AU GENIEVRE

## Calves' Kidneys in Gin

SERVES 4

*75 g/3 oz butter*
*2 calves' kidneys, 400 g/13 oz each, trimmed and*
*pipes removed*
*16 juniper berries*
*100 ml/3½ fl oz dry white wine*
*2 tablespoons gin*
*salt and pepper*

**1** Melt half the butter in a casserole just large enough to take both kidneys. Season the kidneys and brown them on both sides, then cover the casserole and leave them to cook over a very low heat for 25–30 minutes, depending on whether you like them pink or just cooked through.

**2** Crush the juniper berries. Mix the wine and gin together.

**3** When the kidneys are cooked, keep them hot in a covered dish. Remove the cooking fat from the casserole dish, add the wine and gin mixture and deglaze the pot with it, using a wooden spatula to scrape the bottom and sides well. Add the juniper berries and reduce the sauce to a smooth, oily consistency. Add the juices from the kidneys keeping warm and the rest of the butter. Stir again.

**4** Arrange the kidneys on a serving dish, coat them with the sauce and serve them with sautéed or creamed potatoes or a potato gratin.

# GRATIN D'ENDIVES AU JAMBON

## Endive and Ham Gratin

SERVES 3–6

This makes a good starter for six people, or a main course for three.

*6 endives, 125 g/4 oz each*
*100 ml/3½ fl oz milk*
*2 teaspoons cornflour*
*4 pinches grated nutmeg*
*100 g/3½ oz thick* crème fraîche *or 125 ml/4 fl oz*
*double cream*
*75 g/3 oz Emmental cheese, grated*
*6 slices cooked ham, 50 g/2 oz each*
*salt and pepper*

**1** Cut out the small bitter piece at the root end of each endive. Steam the endives for about 10 minutes until the point of a knife can be inserted easily. Drain them and wipe dry.

**2** Preheat the oven to Gas Mark 7/220°C/425°F. Put the cold milk into a milk pan, stir in the cornflour and bring it slowly to the boil over a low heat. Add the salt, pepper and nutmeg and cook for about 2 minutes, still stirring, until the mixture thickens. Add the cream, boil the sauce up for another minute, then remove the pan from the heat. Stir in half the cheese.

**3** Put 3 tablespoons of the cheese sauce into a rectangular oven dish just large enough to hold the endives in a single layer. Wrap each endive in a piece of ham and arrange them head to tail in rows in the oven dish. Coat them with the remaining cheese sauce and top them with the remaining grated cheese.

**4** Transfer the dish to the hot oven to reheat the gratin and brown the top – 15–20 minutes.

# TARTE AU SUCRE
## *Sugar Tart*

SERVES 6

*100 ml/3½ fl oz warm water*
*100 g/3½ oz brown sugar*
*½ packet dried baker's yeast (7 g/¼ oz)*
*75 g/3 oz butter*
*2 eggs*
*250 g/8 oz plain white flour*
*1 pinch salt*
*125 ml/4 fl oz whipping cream*

**1** Put the water and 1 tablespoon of the sugar into a glass which holds 200 ml/7 fl oz. Stir until the sugar has melted, then add the yeast. Stir again and leave to stand for about 10 minutes until the yeast has doubled in volume.

**2** Melt the butter and leave it to cool. Whisk the eggs with a fork. Sieve the flour and salt into a bowl, make a well in the centre, and add the butter, eggs and swollen yeast. Mix with a spatula, then knead with your hands until the dough is supple and no longer sticks to your fingers. Put the dough in a large floured bowl and cover it with a damp cloth. Leave to stand for 1 hour in a warm place, until it has doubled in size.

**3** When the dough has risen, preheat the oven to Gas Mark 7/220°C/425°F. Butter a 26 cm/10-inch tart tin. Knock down the dough with your fist, then line the tin with it by hand. Leave it to stand for 15 minutes, then dust it with the remaining sugar.

**4** Transfer the tart to the centre of the hot oven and leave it to cook for 15 minutes. Then spoon the cream over the top, smoothing it out with the back of the spoon. Put the tart back into the oven and leave it to cook for a further 20–30 minutes until it is golden and covered in a shiny icing.

**5** Slide it out on to a serving dish and serve it warm.

# PAIN PERDU
## *Belgian-style French Toast*

In Flanders they also spread slices of bread with jam, sandwich them together, jam on the inside, and then cook them after dipping into milk and beaten egg.

SERVES 4

*250 ml/8 fl oz milk*
*200 g/7 oz caster sugar*
*6 pinches ground cinnamon*
*4 slices white bread*
*2 eggs*
*75 g/3 oz butter*

**1** Put the milk into a large bowl and add 50 g/2 oz of the sugar and the cinnamon. Stir the mixture and dip the slices of bread into this on each side. Do not leave the bread sitting in the milk or it will break up. Just dip it in.

**2** Whisk the eggs and 50 g/2 oz of the sugar with a fork in a large bowl.

**3** Melt the butter in a large frying pan. Drain the bread and dip it into the beaten egg, coating both sides. Fry the bread in the butter, 3 minutes on each side, until golden.

**4** Drain the bread on kitchen paper, turn it on to a plate, dust it with the remaining sugar and serve it hot.

# DENMARK

## THE FIRST INHABITANTS OF DENMARK

*ate the reindeer, elk, deer and wild oxen which once roamed their forests in*

abundance. When stocks of these became depleted the people moved on to the coast and fed themselves on fish, seabirds and seals. In the Middle Ages they discovered herring, which was to make the country's fortune. It became a staple food, a means of barter, a form of currency, was given as dowries and generally spelt profit. Salted down and smoked, grilled or marinated – there are said to be over 60 ways of serving herring!

Today the Danes grow crops, and raise pigs and cattle too, but they still continue to fish. Their tasty salmon melts in the mouth and is delicious marinated in aniseed and served coated with a sweet mustard sauce: the famous *gravad lax* which is imitated everywhere in the world. But the herring is still the star of Danish cuisine: marinated like salmon; in a curry sauce, *karry sild*; pickled in vinegar, *marinerede sild*; or pan-fried with onions and moistened in dill vinaigrette, *stegt sild i eddike*. In one form or another it appears all the year round

in Nordic dishes of mixed smoked and marinated fish – which include mackerel, eel, lumpfish roe, cod and salmon – served with horseradish cream. It also plays a part in the *kolt bord*, rich buffets composed of as many as 20 deliciously different dishes: herrings, prawn and vegetable salads, marinated cucumber, scrambled egg with smoked eel, bacon omelettes, boiled eggs with lumpfish roe or mustard, meatballs – the famous *frikadeller* – pork liver pâté, parsley chicken, stuffed pork with prunes and apples, brains fritters, caramelised potatoes, steak tartare ... and innumerable desserts, among them apple or raspberry jam gâteaux, cherry flans and fruit jellies. At these festive but informal meals chilled *akuavit* is served – which must be drunk with a toast and an exclamation of '*skål*' – and the national beer, Tuborg or Carlsberg lager, which the little mermaid gave to Copenhagen. Between these feasts there are the *smörrebröd*, literally 'buttered breads', simple, but exquisitely presented.

Round or rectangular slices of bread are spread with butter or margarine and garnished with fish, cheese, eggs, salad, fruit and all kinds of cooked meats. The rye bread canapés topped with one or two slices of liver pâté, a piece of crispy bacon, a slice of tomato, a layer of aspic jelly and a pinch of horseradish are called *smörrebröd Hans Christian Andersen* in honour of the great writer, whose tales still enchant readers of all ages and all nationalities. Denmark is a country of simple, natural cuisine, exquisitely presented.

# AEGGEKAGE

## Egg and Bacon Cake

SERVES 6

*300 g/10 oz thin lean rashers smoked bacon*
*9 eggs*
*2 heaped tablespoons flour*
*200 ml/7 fl oz milk*
*4 tablespoons chopped chives*
*salt and pepper*

**1** Cut the bacon rashers in half across the width and put them into a large non-stick frying pan. Brown them over a gentle heat on both sides, then remove them from the pan and set them aside on a plate lined with kitchen paper.

**2** Using a whisk, beat the eggs in a bowl, incorporating the flour, milk and chives. Season with salt and pepper.

**3** Put the pan in which the bacon was cooked on to a low heat and pour in the beaten egg mixture. Leave it to cook, covered, for 15 minutes, then arrange the bacon on top of the eggs and leave to cook for a further 5 minutes.

**4** Transfer the *aeggekage* to a serving dish and leave it to cool. Serve it with a seasonal salad.

# GRAVADLAX

## Marinated Salmon

In Denmark, as in all Scandinavian countries, this salmon is eaten with a sweetened mustard sauce and, on the feast of St John (24 June), with the first new potatoes.

SERVES 8–10

*1.5 kg/3½ lb piece of salmon*
*4 tablespoons caster sugar*
*4 tablespoons rock salt*
*2 teaspoons crushed peppercorns*
*2 large bunches dill sprigs*

**1** Ask the fishmonger to cut the salmon piece from the part just above the ventral slit, scale it and remove the backbone but not the skin. Rinse and wipe dry the resultant 2 pieces of fish.

**2** Mix the sugar, salt and pepper together in a bowl. Wash and wipe dry the dill. Separate out 10 sprigs. Spread 5 of the sprigs in the bottom of an oven dish and place one piece of salmon, skin side down, on top. Sprinkle the fish with half the mixture from the bowl, then with the bulk of the dill sprigs and finally with the rest of the mixture from the bowl. Put the second piece of fish on top, flesh side down, and place the remaining 5 sprigs of dill on top of that.

**3** Put a lightly weighted plate (with something like a 1 kg/2 lb jar of jam on it) on top of the re-shaped fish and put the dish in the refrigerator. Leave the salmon to marinate for 1–2 days, turning it twice.

**4** At the end of this time, take the fish out of the marinade. Rinse it well and wipe dry. Place the salmon one half at a time on a wooden chopping board, skin side down. Slice the salmon finely, using a very sharp knife and holding the blade almost parallel to the board and without cutting into the skin which will be left whole on the board when you have finished. Arrange the fish on a large serving dish, cover it with clingfilm and keep it in the refrigerator until ready to serve.

**5** Serve it with crispy toast squares or slices of rye bread, lemon quarters, slices of cucumber and new potatoes in their skins.

# MORBRAD MED SVEDSKER OG AEBLER

## *Pork Stuffed with Apple and Prunes*

SERVES 4–6

*1 piece roasting pork, 1.5 kg/3½ lb, boned out and fat removed*
*1 tablespoon coarse rock salt*
*1 tablespoon sugar*
*10 prunes*
*8 walnuts*
*100 g/3½ oz smoked lean bacon*
*4 tablespoons dry white wine*
*1 large apple, e.g. Golden Delicious*
*1 tablespoon oil*
*100 g/3½ oz thick crème fraîche*
*1 tablespoon redcurrant jelly*
*salt and pepper*

**1** Cover the meat with rock salt and sugar, on all sides, and set it aside for 4 hours. Then rinse it and wipe dry.

**2** Prepare the stuffing: stone and chop the prunes. Chop the nuts coarsely. Remove the rind from the bacon. Mince it and brown it in a non-stick frying pan. Away from the heat, add pepper, the chopped nuts, 1 tablespoon of the wine and the chopped prunes. Cut the apple into quarters, peel and core it; chop the flesh and add it to the pan. Stir well.

**3** In order to make a cavity in the meat for the stuffing, make a deep cut across the centre with a big knife, holding the blade almost upright first and then parallel with the work surface, to make a cross shape. Stuff the meat with the mixture, pressing down well and using as much stuffing as possible without it being visible when you have finished.

**4** Lightly oil a large oval gratin dish, just large enough to hold the stuffed meat. Brush the meat with oil and put it into the dish. Transfer it to the oven. Set the oven to Gas Mark 8/230°C/450°F and leave the meat to cook for 30 minutes. Then moisten it with the remaining wine. Leave it to cook for a further hour, lowering the temperature to Gas Mark 4/180°C/350°F.

**5** As soon as the meat is cooked, set it aside on a serving dish. Pour the cream and redcurrant jelly into the gratin dish and bring to the boil. Continue to boil the sauce until it turns thick and smooth. Season to taste. Pour it into a sauce-boat and serve it with the pork.

# STEGT KYLLING

## *Parsley Chicken in a Pot*

SERVES 6

*1.75 kg/4 lb chicken, jointed into 12 pieces*
*1 large bunch flat-leaf parsley (about 100 g/3½ oz)*
*1 tablespoon oil*
*50 g/2 oz butter*
*300 g/10 oz thick double cream*
*salt and pepper*

**1** Rinse and wipe dry the chicken pieces. Season them with salt and pepper. Wash the parsley, remove the stalks and chop the leaves finely: you should have about 6 tablespoons of chopped parsley.

**2** Heat the oil in a large round casserole. Add the butter and when it has melted, brown the pieces of chicken on all sides. Season them during cooking. Skim off the cooking fat; then pour in the cream. Add 4 tablespoons of the parsley, mix well and as soon as it comes to the boil, cover the casserole and leave the chicken to simmer for 1–1¼ hours, stirring from time to time.

**3** As soon as the pieces of chicken are cooked, take them out and set them aside in a deep dish. Reduce the cooking liquid for 2–3 minutes over a low heat, until it becomes smooth and oily in texture. Put the pieces of chicken back into the sauce and stir well. Add the remaining parsley, stir again and turn it out into the deep serving dish. Serve immediately with caramelised potatoes (page 60).

# FRIKADELLER

## *Fricadelles*

SERVES 6

*500 g/1 lb minced veal*
*500 g/1 lb minced pork*
*1 egg, beaten*
*zest of ½ lemon*
*1 small onion*
*2 tablespoons oil*
*salt and pepper*

**1** Prepare the fricadelles: put the two kinds of mince into a large bowl and add the egg, lemon zest, salt and pepper. Very finely chop the onion or grate it with a cylindrical grater. Add it to the meat mixture.

**2** Mix well, then, with the palms of your hands, form the mixture into round shapes 10 x 5 x 2.5 cm/ 4 x 2 x 1 inches in size. This is easiest if you wet your hands in between each fricadelle.

**3** Heat the oil in a large non-stick frying pan. Add the fricadelles and cook them for 10 minutes over a low heat, turning them once half-way through cooking.

**4** When the fricadelles are cooked, arrange them on a serving dish and serve them immediately with braised red cabbage (page 60) or caramelised potatoes (page 60).

# LEVERPOSTEJ

## *Liver Pâté*

SERVES 8

*500 g/1 lb pork liver*
*500 ml/18 fl oz milk*
*100 g/3½ oz onions*
*1 tablespoon oil*
*250 g/8 oz unsmoked belly of pork*
*3 eggs*
*250 g/8 oz thick* crème fraîche
*2 teaspoons flour*
*½ teaspoon mixed spice*
*2 tablespoons brandy*
*salt and pepper*

**1** Rinse and wipe dry the liver and cut it into 4 cm/ 1½-inch pieces. Put it into a bowl, pour the milk over it and leave it to stand for 12 hours in the refrigerator.

**2** At the end of this time, chop the onions. Heat the oil in a non-stick frying pan and just soften the onions in this until they turn golden. Remove the pan from the heat and leave the onions to cool.

**3** Preheat the oven to Gas Mark 6/200°C/400°F. Cut the belly of pork into large cubes, removing the rind. Drain the liver and put it into a food processor or fine mincer bowl. Add the pork and the onion and process the mixture finely.

**4** Break the eggs into a bowl; whisk in the cream and flour. Add salt, pepper, the mixed spice and the brandy. Pour this mixture into the food processor or mincer bowl and blend for a few seconds until all the ingredients are well mixed together.

**5** Oil the bottom and sides of a 25 cm/10-inch oblong pâté terrine and pour in the mixture. Smooth the top with a spatula and cover the pâté with aluminium foil, pierced with a few knife holes.

**6** Place the terrine in a bain-marie (a large shallow pan, such as a roasting tin, filled with hot water to within 2.5 cm/1 inch of the top) and transfer it to the hot oven. Leave it to cook for 1½ hours, until the blade of a knife inserted in the centre of the pâté comes out dry. Allow it to cool and then refrigerate it until ready to serve. This terrine may be made 48 hours in advance.

# DENMARK

Aeblekage
*(Apple Cake)*

Rodgrod
*(Red Fruit Compôte)*

Riz à l'Amande
*(Rice Pudding with Almonds)*

# BRUNEDE KARTOFLER

## *Caramelised Potatoes*

SERVES 6

*1.1 kg/2½ lb small new potatoes*
*100 g/3½ oz sugar*
*4 drops lemon juice*
*100 g/3½ oz butter*
*salt*

**1** Scrub the potatoes under running water and put them in a large saucepan. Cover them with water and bring to the boil. Add salt and leave the potatoes to cook for about another 15 minutes, until they are tender enough for the point of a knife to be inserted into them easily.

**2** As soon as the potatoes are cooked, drain them, leave them to cool and then peel them. Rinse and dry the saucepan.

**3** Put the sugar into the saucepan. Add 3 tablespoons of water and the lemon juice and place the pan on a low heat. Leave to cook until the mixture becomes an amber-coloured caramel. Add the butter and stir well. Drop the potatoes in and cook them for a further 2–3 minutes, turning them frequently in the caramel to coat them evenly. Serve the potatoes immediately.

# RODKAL

## *Braised Red Cabbage*

SERVES 6

*1 red cabbage, 1 kg/2 lb*
*25 g/1 oz butter*
*1 heaped tablespoon caster sugar*
*3 tablespoons water*
*2 tablespoons red wine vinegar*
*2 tablespoons redcurrant jelly*
*salt and pepper*

**1** Remove the outer leaves from the cabbage, cut the rest into quarters vertically and remove the stalk. Cut each cabbage quarter into fine slices.

**2** Put the butter, sugar, water and vinegar in a large round casserole. Add salt and pepper and bring it to the boil. Add the cabbage and stir well. Cover the casserole with a lid and leave the cabbage to simmer for 1¼ hours over a very low heat, stirring from time to time.

**3** When the cabbage is cooked, add the redcurrant jelly to the pan and stir until the jelly has melted – about 10 minutes.

**4** Serve the cabbage hot as an accompaniment to poultry or any roast meat.

# RIS A L'AMANDE

## *Rice Pudding with Almonds*

This delicious pudding is sometimes served with a strawberry or cherry *coulis*, or sometimes with maraschino cherries.

SERVES 6

*500 ml/18 fl oz water*
*250 g/8 oz short-grain rice*
*1 litre/1 ¾ pints milk*
*1 vanilla pod*
*200 g/7 oz caster sugar*
*200 g/7 oz chopped almonds*
*200 ml/7 fl oz whipping cream, chilled*

1 Boil up the water in a saucepan and pour in the rice. Leave it to boil for 10 minutes; then drain it.

2 Pour the milk into a large saucepan and add the vanilla pod, broken in two. Bring the milk to the boil and add the rice. Once the milk has returned to the boil, leave the rice to cook on a low heat for 20 minutes, stirring frequently, until it is very soft. Then add the sugar and stir until it has melted.

3 Leave the rice to cool, then remove the vanilla pod halves and add the almonds. Mix well and leave the pudding to stand in the refrigerator for a minimum of 1 hour.

4 When you are ready to serve the pudding, whip the cream until it forms peaks between the spikes of a fork and fold it into the rice pudding. Serve immediately in a pretty glass serving dish.

# AEBLEKAGE

## *Apple Cake*

SERVES 6

*1 kg/2 lb apples, sweet and tasty variety*
*175 g/6 oz plain flour*
*100 g/3½ oz caster sugar*
*1 teaspoon ground cinnamon*
*125 g/4 oz butter*

1 Preheat the oven to Gas Mark 6/200°C/400°F. Butter a deep 25 cm/10-inch loose-based cake tin.

2 Cut the apples into quarters, peel them and cut them into 4 again, removing the core. Cut each piece into 3 strips and spread them out in the tin.

3 Put the flour in a bowl, make a well in the centre and put in the sugar, cinnamon and butter. Work the mixture by hand until it is of a rough crumble consistency. Sprinkle the mixture over the apples. Transfer the tin to the oven and leave the cake to cook for 40 minutes until it is golden.

4 When the cake is cooked, carefully transfer it from the tin to a plate and serve it cold or warm, with custard or whipped cream.

# RODGROD

## *Red Fruit Compôte*

This dessert is very popular in Denmark, where it is made in July and August, using all the red fruit available, the mix varying according to what is in the market.

SERVES 6

*1 kg/2 lb mixed red fruit: strawberries, raspberries, redcurrants, wild strawberries, cherries, etc.*
*500 ml/18 fl oz water*
*2 teaspoons arrowroot powder, diluted in 100 ml/3½ fl oz water*
*100 g/3½ oz sugar*

1 Pick over the fruit, discarding the stalks. Wash the fruit, and place it in a large saucepan. Add the water and bring it to the boil. Simmer for 1 minute, gently stirring, and then drain the fruit, reserving the cooking juice in the saucepan.

2 Add the diluted arrowroot to the saucepan with the sugar. Stir, and leave the juice to boil up for 3–4 minutes until it thickens. Put the fruit back in, stir and remove the pan from the heat.

3 Turn the compôte out into a glass serving bowl and leave it to cool. Leave it to stand in the refrigerator for 2 hours before serving.

4 Serve it with cream if wished, whipped or pouring, and with chopped toasted almonds.

# SPAIN

*CAN ONE REALLY TALK ABOUT A SPANISH CUISINE,*
*given that the country is divided into large areas, regions which are*

themselves split up into several provinces, each one with its own produce and its own indigenous recipes? Generally speaking though, all Spaniards like cooking with olive oil, and enjoy dishes that are strong tasting and highly coloured, flavoured with garlic, saffron and red peppers. They eat lunch late and dinner very late and love to nibble between meals or to replace a meal with snacks known as 'tapas', eaten standing up in some bar, well before midday or well after midnight. In Barcelona typical tapas are prawns *a la plancha*, spiced seafood, and tiny helpings of Catalan dishes washed down with the sweet white wines of Panades or the aromatic wines of Priorato. In the Basque country, *jamon serrano, lomo*, tuna salad with mayonnaise – created in Minorca in 1756 – and *piquillos* stuffed with cod are eaten with a delicious chilled Txacoli. In Madrid tapas usually include more cooked dishes: meat and fish croquettes and fritters, *empanadillas, angullas*, Salamanca and chorizo sausages are served

with the light wines of Galicia and the rougher reds and whites of Rioja as well as pastis or beer. Andalusian tapas include some of the best ham in the world: *jamon jabugo pata negra*, served with bread rubbed with tomato and olive oil, marinated anchovies, chicken or cod croquettes, squid fritters and all kinds of tasty seafood fried in olive oil – all finer delicacies than one might think. And the delicious and light *jerez fino* and *manzanilla* flow freely in the sunlight all along the Guadalquivir.

These delicious snacks cannot replace the great dishes of Spain however: the Andalusian *gazpacho* and *salmonejo; paella Valenciana;* Basque *marmitako, kokotxas, calamares* and *bacalao; cocido madrileño;* Aragon chicken *chilindro* – with green pepper, onion, tomato and chilli sauce – or Catalan *zarzuela de mariscos.* These are dishes as tasty and exuberant as the Sevillians, as colourful as the *feria* costumes, as lingering as the flamenco, never forgotten when once you have tasted them in their native land.

# BACALAO A LA VIZCAINA

## *Cod Basque-style*

SERVES 4

*500 g/1 lb salt cod, cut from the thickest part of the
fillet, skinned and boned
2 large red peppers
250 g/8 oz onions
4 tablespoons olive oil
salt and pepper*

**1** Twenty-four hours before making this dish, cut
the cod into 6 cm/2½-inch chunks. Rinse it well
under running water, then leave it to desalinate in
a large quantity of cold water, changing the water
several times.

**2** At the end of 24 hours, drain the cod. Heat the
grill and grill the red peppers, not too close to the
heat, for about 30 minutes, turning frequently,
until the skin is browned and crackly. Leave the
peppers to cool in a covered bowl. Chop the
onions.

**3** When the peppers are cool, remove the skin,
open them up and cut out the core, seeds and white
pith; save the juice that drips from them during this
operation. Cut the peppers into thin strips.

**4** Heat the oil in a buffet casserole. Put in the
onions and cook them for about 10 minutes until
they have just turned golden, stirring continuously.
Add the peppers and stir for 2 minutes. Add the
pepper juice, season with salt and pepper, cover the
casserole and leave to cook for 1 hour on a very low
heat, stirring frequently, until the vegetables are
really mushy.

**5** When the vegetables are cooked, mash them to
a thick sauce consistency in the casserole. Lay the
pieces of cod on top, lightly pressing them into the
sauce, cover the casserole and leave to cook for 30
minutes on a very low heat, turning half-way through
cooking.

**6** When the cod is cooked, divide it between 4
warm plates, coat it with the sauce and serve
immediately, with new potatoes cooked in their
skins.

# MARMITAKO

## *Ragout of Tuna Fish with Potato*

SERVES 4

*1 kg/2 lb tuna fish in the piece, 3 cm/1¼ inches thick
100 g/3½ oz onions
250 g/8 oz ripe tomatoes
2 garlic cloves
750 g/1½ lb small new potatoes
4 tablespoons olive oil
1 tablespoon chopped flat-leaf parsley
salt and pepper*

**1** The slice of tuna must be cut from the middle of
the fish, just after the ventral slit. Skin the fish and
remove the backbone and the brown parts around
it: this will give you 4 triangular pieces of well-
trimmed tuna. Wash it, wipe dry and dust with salt.
Allow it to stand for 20 minutes.

**2** Meanwhile, finely chop the onions. Scald the
tomatoes in boiling water for 10 seconds, cool
them under cold running water, skin, halve and de-
seed them; roughly chop the flesh. Finely chop the
garlic cloves. Peel the potatoes, wash them and
wipe dry.

**3** Heat the oil in a large round casserole. Put in the
garlic and parsley mixed together and stir for 2
minutes. Add the onion and cook for 3 minutes,
until it has just turned golden. Add the tomatoes
and potatoes and stir again. Pour in enough water
to just come up to the level of the potatoes. Season
with salt and pepper, cover the casserole and leave
the vegetables to cook for 5 minutes.

**4** Rinse the pieces of fish and wipe them dry. Add
them to the casserole. Leave to cook for a further
5 minutes, still covered and on a low heat. Then
turn the tuna over and cook the other side for a
further 10 minutes.

**5** When the tuna ragout is cooked, remove the lid
and bring it to the table in the cooking pot. Serve
immediately.

# ZARZUELA

## *Fish Stew*

A typical dish from the north-west coast of Spain, this soup may also be made with a mixture of shellfish.

SERVES 6

*1 piece monkfish, 500 g/1 lb, cut from the tail end*
*1 bream, 500 g/1 lb*
*500 g/1 lb cod or haddock*
*250 g/8 oz squid*
*300 g/10 oz large prawns*
*500 g/1 lb fresh mussels*
*500 g/1 lb ripe tomatoes*
*3 garlic cloves*
*200 g/7 oz onions*
*6 tablespoons olive oil*
*2 bay leaves*
*4 parsley stalks*
*200 ml/7 fl oz dry white wine*
*salt and pepper*

**1** Ask the fishmonger to gut and scrub the fish and cut them into 3 cm/1¼-inch thick steaks. Wash the squid, clean them and use only the tentacles and body, chopped into rings (page 93). Wash the prawns and wipe dry. Scrub the mussels, remove their beards, rinse them and wipe dry. Discard any mussels that are cracked or shells that are open and do not close when sharply tapped.

**2** Scald the tomatoes in boiling water for 10 seconds, cool them under cold running water, peel, halve and de-seed them and roughly chop the flesh. Chop the garlic and onion.

**3** Heat the oil in a large round cocotte. Put in the chopped onion and garlic and stir for 3 minutes on a low heat. Add the tomatoes, bay leaves, parsley stalks, salt and pepper. Mix well and pour on the wine. Allow to evaporate over a high heat.

**4** Put the squid into the cocotte. Add the monkfish, cod and bream. Cover them with water and place the cocotte on a high heat. Bring to the boil, cover the cocotte and cook the fish for 5 minutes. Add the prawns and cook them for a further 3 minutes, still covered. Finally, add the mussels to the pot and cook them for 3 minutes, which is the time it takes them to open. Discard any that do not.

**5** Take the fish and shellfish out of the cocotte and arrange them in a tureen. Boil the cooking liquid hard for 5 minutes, then put it into the tureen. Remove the bay leaf and parsley stalks. Serve immediately with crispy toast.

# GAMBAS AL AJILLO

## *Prawns in Garlic*

SERVES 4

*24 raw giant prawns, shelled*
*4 garlic cloves*
*4 tablespoons olive oil*
*1 small dried chilli*
*salt*

**1** Rinse and wipe dry the prawns. Cut the garlic cloves into fine slivers.

**2** Heat the oil in a large frying pan. Put in the garlic and crumble in the chilli. Stir for 30 seconds, then add the prawns. Seal them on a high heat for 2 minutes, turning continuously. Season with salt during cooking.

**3** Divide the prawns between 4 hot plates and serve them immediately with saffron rice (page 69).

# BULLINADA

A Catalan dish.

SERVES 6

*1.5 kg/3½ lb mixed white fish, e.g. monkfish, bass, bream, etc.*
*1 kg/2 lb new potatoes*
*4 garlic cloves*
*6 tablespoons olive oil*
*3 tablespoons chopped flat-leaf parsley*
*6 pinches saffron strands*
*4 pinches cayenne pepper*
*approx. 1 litre/1¾ pints fish stock*
*salt and pepper*

**1** Ask your fishmonger to clean, scale and fillet the fish. Peel, wash and cut the potatoes into 3 mm/

⅛-inch slices. Finely chop the garlic cloves.

**2** Heat the oil in a large round casserole. Put in the garlic, parsley, saffron, cayenne pepper, salt and pepper and stir for 2 minutes on a medium heat, until the garlic turns golden.

**3** Remove the casserole from the heat and spread a layer of potato in the bottom, followed by a layer of fish, and continue until all is used. Finish with a layer of fish. Pour on the fish stock: it should come up to the level of the top layer of fish. Put the casserole back on to a high heat. Bring to the boil, reduce the heat, cover the casserole and leave to simmer for 15 minutes.

**4** When the soup is cooked, remove the lid and bring it to the table in the casserole. Serve it in deep dishes with garlic toast coated with olive oil.

# ALMEJAS A LA MARINERA

## *Clams in White Wine and Tomatoes*

This recipe can also be made using mussels.

SERVES 4

*4 dozen clams*
*200 ml/7 fl oz dry white wine*
*1 small onion*
*2 garlic cloves*
*250 g/8 oz just ripe tomatoes*
*50 g/2 oz white bread (with the crusts cut off)*
*1 hard-boiled egg*
*3 tablespoons olive oil*
*2 tablespoons chopped flat-leaf parsley*

**1** Rinse the clams and put them in a large round cocotte. Pour in the wine and bring to the boil. Leave to cook until the clams open, stirring with a slotted spoon. Then drain them in a colander over a bowl. Discard any clams that haven't opened. Strain the juice through a sieve over a second bowl. Rinse and wipe dry the cocotte.

**2** Chop the onion and garlic finely. Scald the tomatoes in boiling water for 10 seconds, cool them under cold running water, cut them in half and de-seed them. Chop the flesh finely. Grate the

bread to give fine breadcrumbs. Shell the egg; dice the white finely and break up the yolk with a fork.

**3** Heat the oil in the cocotte and add the garlic and onion. Stir for 3 minutes until they are turning golden, then add the tomato. Stir for 2 minutes over a high heat, then pour in the mixture of wine and clam juice. Allow to boil until the liquid reduces by half, then add the breadcrumbs and egg yolk. Stir well. Put the clams back in the cocotte to reheat them and coat them with the sauce. Sprinkle the egg white and parsley in, stir and serve immediately.

# TORTILLA DE PATATA

## *Potato Omelette*

Spanish omelettes are always round and thick; they are eaten at any time of day and are a star ingredient in a selection of tapas.

SERVES 4–6

*500 g/1 lb potatoes, floury variety*
*1 small onion*
*6 tablespoons olive oil*
*6 eggs*
*salt and pepper*

**1** Peel, wash and cut the potatoes into slices 3 mm/⅛-inch thick. Finely chop the onion.

**2** Pour 100 ml/3½ fl oz of water into a medium-size non-stick frying pan and add 3 tablespoons of the olive oil. Bring to the boil and put in the potatoes. Stir, season with salt, cover the pan and leave the potatoes to cook for 12 minutes, turning them frequently; they must be just cooked. Add the chopped onion and stir for a further 3 minutes.

**3** Break the eggs into a bowl and beat them with salt, pepper and the remaining oil. Pour this over the potatoes and as soon as the egg starts to solidify, smooth over the surface and cover the pan. Cook for 6 minutes, then turn out the omelette upside down on a lightly oiled plate. Slide it back into the pan and cook the second side for a further 8 minutes, still covered.

**4** Transfer the omelette to a serving dish and eat it warm or cold, cut into squares or wedges.

# SPAIN

Tortilla de Patate
*(Potato Omelette)*

Gambas al Ajillo
*(Prawns in Garlic)*

Crema Catalana
*(Catalan Cream)*

## Sopa de Ajo

### *Garlic Soup*

This type of soup is found throughout Spain; this particular version is typical of Madrid.

SERVES 4

*4 garlic cloves*
*100 g/3½ oz white bread (with crusts cut off)*
*4 tablespoons olive oil*
*½ teaspoon mild paprika*
*4 pinches cayenne pepper*
*1 litre/1¾ pints chicken or vegetable stock*
*4 eggs*
*salt*

**1** Cut the garlic cloves into fine slivers. Reduce the bread to fine breadcrumbs in a blender or food processor. Heat the oil in a frying pan and fry the garlic and bread in it until they start to turn golden. Add some salt, the paprika and the cayenne pepper powder and mix them in thoroughly. Remove the pan from the heat and divide the contents between 4 soup bowls.

**2** Pour the stock into a large saucepan and bring to the boil. Break the eggs into 4 saucers and drop them carefully into the stock. Cook for 3–4 minutes, carefully basting the egg white over the yolk with a wooden spatula.

**3** Take the eggs out with the spatula and divide them between the 4 soup bowls. Boil up the stock for 1 minute, then strain it over the soup bowls. Serve immediately with slices of crisp toast, with or without garlic and drizzled with olive oil.

## Riñones al Jerez

### *Kidneys in Sherry*

SERVES 4

*2 calves' kidneys, 400 g/13 oz each, trimmed and de-piped*
*200 g/7 oz onions*
*4 tablespoons olive oil*
*200 ml/7 fl oz dry sherry*
*salt and pepper*

**1** Cut the kidneys in half lengthwise and then into 15 mm/⅝-inch strips. Finely chop the onions.

**2** Heat the oil in a round gratin dish or frying pan. Put in the onions and stir them for 5 minutes on a low heat, until they just turn golden. Add the kidneys and brown them on a high heat on both sides for about 3 minutes, stirring continuously.

**3** Pour the sherry into the dish and allow it to evaporate on a high heat, still stirring continuously. Season with salt and pepper. Cover the dish and leave to cook for 5 minutes on a very low heat.

**4** Arrange the kidneys on a serving dish, coat them with the cooking juices and serve. Saffron rice (page 69) goes well with this dish.

# Cocido Madrileño

## *Madrid-style Stew*

This dish is from the Madrid area. Originally known as *l'olla podrida* (the poor man's meal), it was made using any available meat and vegetables.

SERVES 8

*400 g/13 oz chick-peas*
*2 carrots*
*1 leek*
*1 onion*
*1 oven-ready chicken, 2 kg/4½ lb*
*1 kg/2 lb rib of beef, on the bone*
*250 g/8 oz piece of smoked bacon*
*250 g/8 oz piece of salted bacon*
*250 g/8 oz piece of cooked ham*
*200 g/7 oz chorizo sausage*
*1 green cabbage heart*
*8 small potatoes, firm variety*
*salt*

**1** Put the chick-peas into a large casserole dish and cover them generously with water. Leave them to soak for 12 hours.

**2** At the end of this time, drain the chick-peas and put them into a very large round casserole. Peel the carrots and leek. Cut them in half and add them to the casserole with the onion.

**3** Rinse the chicken, rib of beef, bacon and ham. In a separate pan, boil them up for 5 minutes, then drain them and rinse again; put them into the casserole, on top of the chick-peas. Cover generously with water and bring to the boil. Leave to simmer for 2 hours.

**4** Meanwhile, prick the chorizo a few times with a fork and put it into a saucepan. Add enough water to just cover it and bring to the boil. Leave it to simmer for 10 minutes, then pour off the water. Cut the cabbage into quarters. Peel, rinse and wipe dry the potatoes.

**5** At the end of 2 hours' cooking, add the chorizo to the casserole with the cabbage and potatoes. Add more water if necessary, to cover the meat and vegetables. Leave to cook on a low heat for a further hour, covered. Season with salt during cooking.

**6** When the meat and vegetables are cooked, remove them with a slotted spoon. Put the chick-peas, cabbage and potatoes on one dish and the meat on another. Serve hot. You can strain the cooking broth and cook some vermicelli in it. It can then be served as a first course.

# Arroz con Azafrán

## *Saffron Rice*

This rice is excellent as an accompaniment to dishes with a sauce or gravy and also with grills and roasts.

SERVES 4

*150 g/5 oz onions*
*3 tablespoons olive oil*
*300 g/10 oz long-grain rice*
*4 pinches saffron strands*
*900 ml/1½ pints boiling water*
*salt and pepper*

**1** Finely chop the onions.

**2** Put the oil into a large saucepan. Place it on a low heat and put in the onions. Stir well. Add 100 ml/3½ fl oz of water. Cover the pan and leave to cook for 5–6 minutes until the water has evaporated and the onions have just turned golden.

**3** Add the rice and saffron. Stir for 2 minutes over a medium heat to lightly colour the rice. Pour on the boiling water. Season with salt and pepper and stir. Cover the pan and leave to cook for about 20 minutes, without touching, until the rice has absorbed all the water.

**4** When the rice is cooked, stir it with a fork to loosen up the grains. Turn it out into a deep dish and serve.

# COCHIFRITO

## *Fricassée of Lamb with Garlic*

SERVES 6

*1.25 kg/3 lb shoulder of lamb, boned out and*
*trimmed of fat*
*4 garlic cloves*
*100 g/3½ oz onions*
*3 tablespoons olive oil*
*2 pinches caster sugar*
*2 tablespoons lemon juice*
*4 pinches cayenne pepper*
*1 teaspoon mild paprika*
*2 tablespoons chopped flat-leaf parsley*
*100 ml/3½ fl oz meat or vegetable stock*
*salt and pepper*

**1** Cut the meat into 3 cm/1¼-inch cubes. Season it
with salt and pepper. Finely chop the garlic and
onions.

**2** Heat the oil in a large round cocotte. Put in the
meat and brown it on all sides. Then take it out of
the cocotte and remove the fat from cooking. Put
in the garlic, onion and sugar and stir for 5 minutes
until the onion caramelises. Add the lemon juice,
cayenne pepper, paprika and parsley, the juices
from the meat and the stock. Stir well.

**3** Put the meat back in and stir again. Cover the
cocotte and leave the fricassee to cook on a very low
heat for 1½ hours, until the meat is tender.

**4** Remove the pieces of meat with a slotted spoon
and arrange them in a warmed serving dish. Allow
the cooking liquids to reduce for 5 minutes on a
high heat, until they turn syrupy. Coat the meat
with this sauce and serve immediately with saffron
rice (page 69) or boiled potatoes.

# CONEJO CON ARROZ

## *Rabbit with Rice*

SERVES 6

*1 rabbit, 1.25 kg/3 lb, jointed into 8 pieces*
*2 tablespoons coarse rock salt*
*75 g/3 oz smoked bacon*
*1 onion*
*300 g/10 oz ripe tomatoes*
*3 tablespoons olive oil*
*4 pinches saffron strands*
*750 ml/1¼ pints chicken stock*
*300 g/10 oz long-grain rice*
*salt and pepper*

**1** Rinse and wipe dry the rabbit pieces. Put them
into a casserole, add the rock salt, stir well and leave
to stand for 30 minutes. Then rinse them and wipe
dry.

**2** Finely chop the bacon and the onion. Scald the
tomatoes in boiling water for 10 seconds, cool
them under cold running water; skin, halve and de-
seed them and roughly chop the flesh.

**3** Heat the oil in a large round casserole and brown
the pieces of rabbit on all sides for about 15
minutes. Take the rabbit out of the casserole and
remove the cooking oil. Put the onion and bacon
into the casserole and stir them for 2 minutes over
a low heat until they just turn golden. Add the
tomatoes, saffron, salt and pepper and stir for a
further 3 minutes. Put the pieces of rabbit back in
and pour on the stock. Bring to the boil, cover the
casserole and leave the rabbit to cook on a low heat
for 30 minutes.

**4** At the end of this time, pour the rice in a stream
into the casserole, all around the rabbit pieces.
Cover again and leave to cook for a further 30
minutes until the rice is tender. Serve hot, taking
the casserole dish to the table.

# HABAS CON JAMÓN

## *Broad Beans Catalan-style*

SERVES 4

*1 kg/2 lb fresh broad beans*
*100 g/3½ oz Parma ham, in 2 slices*
*1 onion*
*3 tablespoons olive oil*
*salt and pepper*

**1** Shell the beans, removing the little bitter tops. Cut the ham into 1 cm/½-inch cubes. Finely chop the onion.

**2** Heat the oil in a large saucepan. Put in the ham and onion and cook until they turn golden, about 3 minutes, stirring continuously. Add the beans and 3 tablespoons of water. Lightly season with salt, stir, cover the pan and leave to cook for 25 minutes on a low heat, turning from time to time.

**3** Turn the beans out into a deep dish, season with pepper and serve immediately.

# POLLO EN PEPITORIA

## *Chicken with Almonds*

SERVES 6

*1 large onion*
*1 garlic clove*
*25 g/1 oz pine kernels*
*50 g/2 oz blanched almonds*
*1 tablespoon chopped flat-leaf parsley*
*4 pinches saffron strands*
*1 chicken, 1.5 kg/3½ lb, jointed into 8 pieces*
*3 tablespoons olive oil*
*100 ml/3½ fl oz dry white wine*
*2 hard-boiled eggs*
*salt and pepper*

**1** Roughly chop the onion and garlic clove. Put them into a blender or food processor bowl with the pine kernels, almonds, parsley and saffron. Process to a fine purée.

**2** Rinse and wipe dry the chicken pieces. Season them with salt and pepper. Heat the oil in a large oval cocotte. Cook the chicken pieces for 15 minutes to brown them on all sides, then take them out of the cocotte and remove the cooking fat.

**3** Pour the wine into the cocotte and cook until half the liquid has evaporated, deglazing cooking juices by scraping the sides and bottom of the cocotte with a wooden spatula. Add the purée from the blender, stir, and then put the pieces of chicken back in. Mix well to coat the chicken with the purée and wine mixture, cover the cocotte and leave to cook for 1¼ hours on a low heat, turning the chicken pieces from time to time.

**4** At the end of this time, shell the eggs and cut the whites into small cubes. Crumble the yolks with a fork, adding 3 tablespoons of the chicken cooking liquid. Pour this into the cocotte and stir well so the sauce becomes smooth and oily. Add the egg whites, stir and remove from the heat.

**5** Arrange the chicken in a deep dish and serve immediately with the sauce poured over. Serve with saffron rice (page 69).

# Leche Frita

## *Fried Curd*

SERVES 6

*750 ml/1¼ pints milk*
*150 g/5 oz caster sugar*
*zest of 1 unwaxed orange*
*zest of 1 unwaxed lemon*
*1 cinnamon stick*
*75 g/3 oz cornflour or arrowroot*
*4 tablespoons flour*
*1 egg*
*3 tablespoons groundnut oil*
*½ teaspoon ground cinnamon*

**1** Put the milk into a medium-size saucepan. Add 125 g/4 oz of the sugar, the zest of orange and lemon and the cinnamon stick. Add the arrowroot or cornflour and stir. Bring to the boil and cook, stirring continuously, until the mixture thickens. Remove the curd from the heat, leave it to go cold, then take out the citrus zests and the cinnamon stick.

**2** Turn the curd out into a dish which is 10 x 20 cm/4 x 8 inches and 2 cm/¾ inch deep. Leave to stand in a cold place for 4 hours.

**3** At the end of this time, cut the curd into 4 cm/1½-inch squares. Put the flour in a bowl and beat the egg in a second bowl. Dip the curd squares quickly in first the flour and then the egg.

**4** Heat the oil in a large non-stick frying pan. Brown the curd squares in this, 2 minutes each side, and drain them on kitchen paper.

**5** Mix the remaining sugar with the cinnamon and dip the curd squares in this. Eat them immediately.

# Quesada

## *Cheesecake*

SERVES 6

*750 g/1½ lb half-fat soft white cheese*
*3 eggs*
*250 g/8 oz sugar*
*100 g/3½ oz plain flour*
*grated zest of 1 unwaxed lemon*
*½ teaspoon ground cinnamon*
*½ teaspoon vanilla essence*
*a little vanilla sugar*

**1** Preheat the oven to Gas Mark 4/180°C/350°F. Butter a 25 cm/10-inch oval gratin dish.

**2** Beat the cheese with a balloon whisk, incorporating the eggs, sugar, flour, zest of lemon, cinnamon and vanilla essence. Pour the mixture into the gratin dish and transfer it to the oven. Leave the cheesecake to cook for 50 minutes. Then remove it from the oven and dust it with a little vanilla sugar. Leave it to go cold before serving it from its cooking dish.

# TOCINO DE CIELO

## *Heavenly Egg Flan*

Many Spanish desserts are based on egg yolks. These desserts were invented by nuns, who were made regular presents of leftover egg yolks by the sherry makers, who used the whites to clarify their wine.

SERVES 4

*200 g/10 oz caster sugar*
*8 egg yolks*
*½ teaspoon vanilla essence*

**1** Put 150 ml/¼ pint of water into a medium-size saucepan. Add the sugar and bring to the boil. Leave to cook until a drop of the syrup dropped in a glass of cold water will form a little ball, which stays on the bottom of the glass. Brush the base and sides of 4 individual soufflé dishes, 9 cm/3½ inches in diameter, with a little syrup.

**2** Beat the egg yolks by hand, incorporating the hot syrup and whisking continuously. Add the vanilla and give one last stir.

**3** Divide the mixture between the soufflé dishes and arrange them on the perforated part of a steamer. Leave to cook over simmering water for 15 minutes, uncovered.

**4** Leave the little flans to go completely cold before turning them out on to plates. Serve them either at room temperature or chilled.

# CREMA CATALANA

## *Catalan Cream*

SERVES 6

*40 g/1½ oz cornflour or arrowroot*
*1 litre/1¾ pints milk*
*zest of 1 unwaxed lemon*
*1 cinnamon stick*
*1 vanilla pod*
*6 egg yolks*
*300 g/10 oz caster sugar*

**1** Mix the cornflour smoothly in 150 ml/¼ pint of the milk. Pour the rest of the milk into a medium-size saucepan and add the lemon zest, cinnamon and vanilla. Bring to the boil, then remove from the heat and leave to infuse for 10 minutes.

**2** Beat the egg yolks with 200 g/7 oz of the sugar in another medium-size saucepan. Strain in the milk and heat it on a low heat, stirring continuously. Add the blended cornflour and continue to stir until the mixture thickens. Leave it to go cold, then pour it into 6 individual egg plates 15 cm/6 inches in diameter. Leave them to stand in the refrigerator for about 2 hours.

**3** When you are ready to serve the cream, heat the grill. Sprinkle the remaining sugar over the top of the dishes. Slide them under the grill, close to the heat so the sugar caramelises. Serve immediately.

# PORTUGAL

*PORTUGUESE NAVIGATORS WERE THE FIRST
to conquer the seas: in 1497 Vasco de Gama began his voyages to India*

which opened up the sea route from western Europe to the East via the Cape of Good Hope. From the far countries they colonised, Portuguese caravelles brought back their precious cargoes of spices, mild and hot chillis, tea, coffee, rice and fruit. Portugal faces out to sea like a promontory (Cabo da Roca is the most westerly point in Europe), and although its climate is variable, it is always dry and hot in the summer. A great number of exotic plants acclimatised well: yams and pineapples in the Azores, papayas, mangoes, bananas and *maracujas* in Madeira.

Over the centuries the country went through periods of prosperity and with such an abundance of ingredients to add to the local produce its cuisine evolved rapidly. The Portuguese already had the harvest from the sea: fish from the Atlantic coast, from Porto to Lisbon, from which they make their *caldeiradas*, and from the Algarve where they cook shellfish as nowhere else on earth. The climate of their pastures, concentrated in the north-east, the

mountain region, is suited to producing raw and smoked hams and all kinds of sausages. The flat, open country to the east of Lisbon also produces excellent pork, as well as game and freshwater fish. The north-west is the country of *caldo verde*, of duck with rice and of tripe Porto-style. In the Alentejo area, south of Lisbon, meat and shellfish are used in the same recipe, as in pork and clam dishes. In some places the great Madeira and port wines enhance such recipes as marinated rabbit or figs coated with almonds and chocolate.

All these regions have one thing in common: an inordinate love of sweet things; favourite among the 200 or so recipes for these being *ovos moles, pudim de amendoas, pao de lo* and other *toucinho de céu*. They also love sardines and cod, the famous *bacalhau*, which in Portugal can be cooked in as many different ways as there are days in the year. Cod, coming from far-off seas, is also a symbol of that adventuring spirit that is still firmly entrenched in the Portuguese.

# CALDO VERDE

## *Potato Soup with Cabbage and Sausage*

The most famous of Portuguese soups, this is traditionally served with cornbread.

SERVES 6

*1 kg/2 lb potatoes, floury variety*
*1 spring cabbage, heart only*
*100 g/3½ oz mild chorizo-type sausage*
*4 tablespoons olive oil*
*salt and pepper*

**1** Peel and wash the potatoes and place them in a large saucepan. Cover them with cold water and bring to the boil. Season with salt and leave to cook for about 20 minutes until they are really tender.

**2** Meanwhile, wash the cabbage and cut it into strips. Blanch it for 1 minute in boiling water, then drain, rinse and drain again. Skin the sausage and cut it into thin slices.

**3** When the potatoes are cooked, drain them and put them through a blender or food processor with a few spoonfuls of the cooking liquid. Blend to a thick, creamy consistency.

**4** Pour the soup into a large round casserole. Season with salt and pepper. Add the cabbage and stir over a low heat for 2 minutes: the cabbage should remain slightly crunchy.

**5** Add the oil, mix well and add the sausage. Leave the soup to heat through for 2 minutes. Stir it again and serve immediately.

# AÇORDA DE COENTROS

## *Bread Soup with Coriander and Egg*

SERVES 4

*150 g/5 oz white unsliced bread*
*4 garlic cloves*
*4 tablespoons roughly chopped coriander leaves*
*1 teaspoon rock salt*
*4 tablespoons olive oil*
*4 eggs*
*1 litre/1¾ pints chicken stock*
*pepper*

**1** Put the crumbled bread and garlic cloves into a food processor or blender and add the coriander, rock salt and oil. Season lightly with pepper. Blend to a fine purée and pour into 4 individual soup bowls.

**2** Break the eggs into a bowl and beat them with a fork. Strain them into another bowl.

**3** Bring the stock to the boil, then pour in the eggs in a thin stream, stirring with a fork: this makes little flakes of egg which float in the soup. Leave the soup to cook for 3 minutes, then pour it into the bowls containing the bread and garlic purée. Serve immediately. Each guest stirs his or her own soup before eating.

# CALDEIRADA
## *Fish and Potato Stew*

This recipe and the next are traditionally made with fresh clams. If these are unobtainable, small clams or Venus clams may be substituted.

SERVES 8

*32 clams*
*100 g/3½ oz onions*
*1 small green pepper*
*2 garlic cloves*
*500 g/1 lb tomatoes*
*6 tablespoons olive oil*
*500 g/1 lb potatoes, floury variety*
*4 pieces cod, 400 g/13 oz in total*
*4 pieces monkfish, 400 g/13 oz in total*
*500 g/1 lb small squid*
*400 ml/14 fl oz dry white wine*
*pepper*

1  Rinse the clams in several changes of cold water and drain them. Finely chop the onions. Wash the green pepper, halve it, remove the core, seeds and white pith and chop the flesh. Finely chop the garlic cloves. Scald the tomatoes in boiling water for 10 seconds, cool them under cold running water, skin, halve and de-seed them; roughly chop the flesh.

2  Heat 2 tablespoons of the oil in a large saucepan and put in the onions, pepper and garlic. Fry them very gently for 5 minutes on a low heat, stirring continuously, until they have just turned golden. Then add the tomatoes and the clams. Leave the shellfish to open, stirring with a slotted spoon, then remove from the heat and turn them out into a colander. Discard any clams that don't open. Reserve the liquid.

3  Peel, rinse and cut the potatoes into 3 mm/⅛-inch slices. Rinse the fish and wipe dry. Clean the squid (page 93) and cut the bodies into very thin rings.

4  Put the remaining oil into a large casserole. Put in a layer of potato, then the monkfish on top, a second layer of potato, followed by the squid, a third layer of potato and a layer of cod. Top with the remaining potato and sprinkle with the wine and the clam juice. Cover the casserole and put it

on a high heat until the liquid boils. Then leave to cook on a reduced heat for 15 minutes before putting in the clams. Leave to cook for another 5 minutes before serving with slices of crispy toast or French bread. Add pepper at the table.

# AMELJOAS NA CATAPLANA
## *Clams with Ham*

'Cataplana' is the name given to the very well-sealed shell-shaped casserole in which this dish is traditionally cooked. The well-fitting lid of a Le Creuset dish will provide almost the same effect.

SERVES 4

*1 kg/2 lb clams*
*100 g/3½ oz smoked ham*
*250 g/8 oz mild chorizo-type sausage, uncooked*
*500 g/1 lb onions*
*250 g/8 oz ripe tomatoes*
*4 tablespoons olive oil*
*½ teaspoon mild paprika*
*6 pinches cayenne pepper*
*100 ml/3½ fl oz dry white wine*
*2 bay leaves*
*2 tablespoons chopped coriander leaves*
*pepper*

1  Rinse the clams in several changes of cold water and drain them. Finely chop the ham. Skin the sausage and crumble the meat. Finely chop the onions. Scald the tomatoes in boiling water for 10 seconds, refresh them under cold running water, skin, halve and de-seed them; roughly chop the flesh.

2  Heat the oil in a buffet casserole. Put in the onions and cook them over a low heat until they just turn golden, stirring continuously. Add the paprika, cayenne pepper and some pepper and stir again for 2 minutes. Add the ham and sausage and stir again for a further 3 minutes. Add the tomatoes, wine, bay leaves and coriander and bring to the boil. Cook over a high heat, stirring continuously, until the wine has evaporated.

3  Put the clams into the casserole, cover it and cook them for 6 to 8 minutes on a high heat, until the clam shells open. Discard any that do not. Serve immediately with garlic bread.

# BACALHUA A GOMES DE SÀ

## *Cod with Potato and Olives*

SERVES 4

*1 kg/2 lb salt cod, cut from the thickest part of the fillet*
*625 g/1¼ lb potatoes*
*500 g/1 lb onions*
*4 garlic cloves*
*4 tablespoons olive oil*
*2 bay leaves, cut in half*
*1 teaspoon mild paprika*
*20 black olives*
*4 hard-boiled eggs*
*2 tablespoons chopped flat-leaf parsley*
*salt and pepper*

**1** Twenty-four hours before making this dish, cut the cod into 6 cm/2½-inch chunks. Rinse it well under cold running water and then leave it to desalinate in a large bowl of cold water, changing the water frequently.

**2** When the cod is no longer salty, put it into a large saucepan and add 1.5 litres/2½ pints of water. Put the pan on a low heat. When the liquid begins to bubble, simmer for 10 minutes, then drain the fish through a colander (not a metal one).

**3** Scrub and rinse the potatoes and put them into a large saucepan. Cover them with cold water and bring to the boil. Season with salt and leave to cook for about 18 minutes or until they are just cooked.

**4** Finely chop the onions and the garlic cloves. Heat the oil in a medium-size saucepan. Put in the garlic, bay leaves and paprika and stir over a low heat for 2 minutes. Season with salt and pepper. Add the onions, cover the pan and leave to cook for 30 minutes on a very low heat, stirring frequently until the onions become a soft purée.

**5** Preheat the oven to Gas Mark 7/220°C/425°F. Flake the fish, removing the skin and any bones. Stone the olives and cut them into quarters. Shell the boiled eggs and cut them into 3 mm/⅛-inch slices.

**6** When the onion is cooked, spread one-third of it on the bottom of a 30 cm/12-inch gratin dish. Cover the onion layer with half the potatoes, then half the cod and half the eggs. Dot with half the olives. Repeat, beginning with the second third of the onion and ending with the last of the onion. Sprinkle in the parsley, transfer the dish to the oven and leave to cook for 20 minutes until the top is lightly browned. Serve hot from the gratin dish.

# SARDINHAS DE CEBOLADA

## *Sardines with Onion*

SERVES 4

*1 kg/2 lb medium-size sardines*
*2 tablespoons rock salt*
*2 tablespoons lemon juice*
*100 g/3½ oz onions*
*250 g/8 oz ripe tomatoes*
*4 tablespoons olive oil*
*2 bay leaves*
*salt and pepper*

**1** Gut, scale, rinse and wipe dry the sardines. Arrange them on a glass dish, and sprinkle them with the rock salt. Pour the lemon juice over them, stir well, and leave the sardines to stand in the refrigerator for 1 hour.

**2** Slice the onions in thin rings. Scald the tomatoes in boiling water for 10 seconds, cool them under cold running water, skin, halve and de-seed them; roughly chop the flesh.

**3** When the sardines are ready, rinse them and wipe dry. Put half the oil into a large round casserole. Lay one-third of the onions and tomatoes in this. Arrange half the sardines on top, head to tail. Cover with the second third of onions and tomatoes. Arrange the remaining sardines on top and cover with the last of the onions and tomatoes. Season each layer with salt as you go along and tuck the bay leaves into the layers. Sprinkle with the remaining oil and cover the casserole.

**4** Put the casserole on a medium heat, and leave it to cook undisturbed for 20 minutes. Serve the sardines hot from the oven dish and sprinkle them with pepper to serve.

PORTUGAL

Ameljoas com Carne de Porco
*(Pork with Clams and Coriander)*

Caldo Verde
*(Potato Soup with Cabbage and Sausage)*

Galinha Mourisca
*(Chicken Moorish-style)*

# GALINHA MOURISCA

## *Chicken Moorish-style*

SERVES 4

*1 chicken, 1.5 kg/3½ lb, jointed into 8 pieces*
*100 g/3½ oz onions*
*100 g/3½ oz slightly salted lean bacon*
*4 tablespoons olive oil*
*2 tablespoons chopped parsley*
*2 tablespoons chopped mint*
*2 tablespoons chopped coriander leaves*
*6 tablespoons lemon juice*
*4 eggs*
*salt and pepper*

**1** Rinse the chicken pieces and wipe dry; season them with salt and pepper. Chop the onions and finely chop the bacon.

**2** Heat the oil in a large oval cocotte and brown the chicken pieces on all sides. Then take them out and put in the bacon, onions and chopped herbs. Season with salt and pepper and cook until they have turned golden, stirring continuously.

**3** Put the chicken pieces back in the cocotte and sprinkle them with the lemon juice. Mix well, lower the heat, cover the cocotte and leave the chicken to cook for 1½ hours, stirring from time to time.

**4** Fifteen minutes before the end of the chicken cooking time, boil the eggs: boil up some water in a saucepan, put the eggs in and cook them for 5 minutes; they will be soft-boiled. Drain them, cool them under cold running water and shell them carefully.

**5** When the chicken pieces are cooked, take them out of the pot and set them aside in a deep dish. Boil up the cooking juices to reduce them to a syrupy consistency and coat the chicken pieces with this. Serve each guest with a piece of chicken in sauce and a soft-boiled egg. When the eggs are cut, the yolk runs out and mixes with the sauce.

# PORCO ASSADO COM LARANJA

## *Roast Pork with Orange*

SERVES 6

*1.25 kg/3 lb pork fillet, trimmed*
*4 garlic cloves*
*1 tablespoon rock salt*
*2 tablespoons olive oil*
*150 ml/¼ pint fresh orange juice*
*3 tablespoons fresh lemon juice*
*1 unwaxed orange*
*pepper*

**1** Ask the butcher to roll and tie up the meat but without adding barding fat. Rinse it and wipe dry. Grind the garlic cloves in a mortar with the rock salt and some pepper. Add the oil. Coat the meat with this, pressing it well on. Mix the orange and lemon juice together.

**2** Preheat the oven to Gas Mark 7/220°C/425°F. Place the meat lengthwise in a gratin dish. Transfer it to the oven and leave to cook for 30 minutes, basting the meat regularly with the orange and lemon juice mixture.

**3** Meanwhile, rinse the orange, wipe it dry and cut it into thin slices. When the meat has been cooking for 30 minutes, turn it over and cover the top with orange slices. Reduce the oven temperature to Gas Mark 4/180°C/350°F and cook for a further 45 minutes.

**4** When the meat is cooked, place it on a serving dish. Reduce the cooking juices on a high heat until syrupy in consistency and pour them into a sauce-boat. Serve hot with rice.

# Ameljoas com Carne de Porco

## *Pork with Clams and Coriander*

This recipe is traditionally made with fresh clams. If these are unobtainable, small clams or Venus clams may be substituted.

SERVES 6

*1 kg/2 lb pork fillet, trimmed*
*6 garlic cloves*
*1 teaspoon rock salt*
*2 tablespoons mild paprika*
*150 ml/¼ pint wine vinegar*
*4 tablespoons chopped coriander leaves*
*1 bay leaf, cut in quarters*
*4 tablespoons olive oil*
*1 kg/2 lb clams*
*1 unwaxed lemon*
*100 g/3½ oz black olives*
*pepper*

**1** Cut the meat into 2 cm/¾-inch cubes. Grind the garlic cloves in a mortar with the rock salt and paprika. Incorporate the vinegar, half the coriander and the bay leaf. Roll the pieces of meat in this mixture and leave them to marinate for 3 hours.

**2** At the end of this time, heat the oil in a large round casserole and brown the meat for 5 minutes, turning it all the time. Add water to a depth of 5 cm/2 inches, cover the casserole and leave to cook for 1¼ hours on a low heat, stirring from time to time.

**3** Meanwhile, rinse the clams in several changes of water and drain them. Put them in with the meat after the 1¼ hours' cooking time. Cook for a further 10 minutes until the shellfish open. Discard any that do not. Cut the lemon into slices and each slice into quarters. Then stir it in with the olives, some pepper and the remaining coriander and serve.

# Pudim de Laranja

## *Orange Puddings*

SERVES 4

*350 ml/12 fl oz fresh orange juice*
*125 g/4 oz caster sugar*
*1 strip unwaxed orange zest*
*2 eggs + 2 egg yolks*

**1** Put the orange juice into a small saucepan, and add the sugar and orange zest. Bring to the boil and allow to boil for 10 minutes, until you have a clear syrup. Take out the orange zest.

**2** Preheat the oven to Gas Mark 3/160°C/325°F. Whisk the whole eggs and egg yolks together quickly in a bowl, by hand or in a blender. Pour in the syrup in a thin trickle, continuing to beat as you do so.

**3** Strain this mixture into 4 ramekins 8 cm/3 inches in diameter. Stand these in a rectangular oven dish or bain-marie and surround them with boiling water to come two-thirds of the way up the ramekins. Transfer the dish to the oven and leave the puddings to cook for 1 hour.

**4** At the end of this time, take the ramekins out of their bain-marie and leave the puddings to go cold. Put them in the refrigerator to chill for 6–12 hours. Serve them in their ramekins.

# PAO-DE-LO

## *Fluffy Lemon Sponge*

This light sponge is traditionally made in big round cake tins.

SERVES 6

*5 eggs*
*150 g/5 oz caster sugar*
*3 tablespoons lemon juice*
*grated zest of 1 lemon*
*125 g/4 oz plain flour*
*1 teaspoon baking powder*
*1 pinch salt*

For the oven dish:
*20 g/¾ oz butter*
*1 tablespoon flour*

**1** Preheat the oven to Gas Mark 3/160°C/325°F. Grease and flour the sides of the dish and line the base with a piece of greaseproof paper.

**2** Separate 3 of the eggs. Put the yolks into one bowl and the whites in another. Add the 2 remaining whole eggs to the bowl with the yolks in and fold in 100 g/3½ oz of the sugar. Beat with an electric whisk for 10 minutes until the mixture turns white and has doubled in volume. Add the lemon juice and zest.

**3** Sieve the flour and baking powder into the egg yolk, sugar and lemon mixture and fold it in with a flexible spatula.

**4** Add the salt to the egg whites and beat them to a firm snow. Incorporate the rest of the sugar, still beating, until the mixture is smooth and shiny. Fold it into the first mixture.

**5** Turn the mixture into the oven dish and put it in the oven. Leave it to cook for 1 hour: the cake will rise considerably and turn golden-coloured. Remove it from the oven and leave it to stand for 10 minutes before turning it out. Serve it cold, in slices. *Pao-de-lo* may be served spread with *ovos moles* (opposite).

# OVOS MOLES

## *Egg Yolk Creams*

SERVES 4

*150 g/5 oz caster sugar*
*1 teaspoon lemon juice*
*1 teaspoon vanilla essence*
*6 egg yolks*
*ground cinnamon, to taste*

**1** Put the sugar into a medium-size saucepan. Add the lemon juice, vanilla and 3 tablespoons of water. Put the saucepan on a medium heat and cook until little bubbles appear on the surface of the resultant syrup. Remove the pan from the heat and leave the syrup to cool.

**2** Beat the egg yolks with a fork, then strain them into the saucepan. Stir with a wooden spoon and put the pot back on to a low heat. Leave to cook for 10 minutes, stirring continuously, until the mixture turns into a smooth, very thick cream.

**3** Divide it between 4 ramekins and leave to go cold. Put them into the refrigerator, and dust with cinnamon when ready to serve.

# NETHERLANDS

*ONCE AGAIN THIS FLAT COUNTRY HAS recently regained land from the sea to cultivate vegetables and tulips and*

increase the harvest. But only 10% of people in the Netherlands are farmers and growers, the rest are industrialists, business people, fishermen: herring fishermen for the most part but they also catch fresh cod, sole, turbot, plaice, eels, prawns, mussels and oysters. They are the descendants of those hardy navigators who left to conquer the world and founded an immense Dutch colonial empire. Since the seventeenth century their cuisine has been influenced by produce imported from the far corners of the earth: sugar, spices, tea and condiments. Hence the popularity of Indonesian dishes in the Dutch menu like *rijstafel, nasigoreng* and *bamigoreng*. Everyday cookery, as well as that for festive occasions, is distinguished by its plain, bracing, country quality: vegetable and split pea soups; meat croquettes and meatballs – *bitterhalen* and *gehaktballen*; potato pancakes – *riftkoekjes*; apples and potatoes cooked with bacon or sausage – *hete bliksem*; *huspot* – a pork stew with potato and carrot; *stampot boerenkool* – cabbage, potato and sausage casserole. Many of their desserts, sweet-

meats and biscuits contain spices. Delicious cheeses from the lovely Dutch dairies are eaten at any time of day with bread and beer and are used in cooking: young or mature Gouda, tender Mimolette, Edam from Alkmaar and the sweet, holey Maasdam.

And to go back to herrings: the Dutch eat these at any time of day too: raw, marinated, salted, preserved by the *cauque* method, a Dutch preserving invention of the seventeenth century, or simply salted and smoked. But only the first spring herrings, caught in May, are eaten raw in the ports, with bread and fresh onion. Salted and smoked herrings are desalinated before being eaten in various ways, according to personal taste. Herrings are so important a factor in the life of the Netherlands that the first catch of the year is a big event and the first fisherman to return with a catch has the privilege of presenting a barrel to the Queen.

The wise Dutch are happy with what they have: excellent, natural and healthy produce which is cooked without fuss or frills. Cooking for them is simply part of the art of living happily.

# Maatjesharing

## Marinated Herrings

SERVES 4

*750 g/1½ lb fresh herrings*
*2 tablespoons coarse rock salt*
*6 tablespoons caster sugar*
*100 g/3½ oz onions*
*200 ml/7 fl oz cider vinegar*
*2 tablespoons coriander seeds*
*6 cloves*
*1 tablespoon coarsely ground pepper*

**1** Trim the heads from the herrings, gut them and split them into fillets, removing the backbones (or get your fishmonger to do this for you). Wash the fish and wipe dry. Mix the rock salt with 2 tablespoons of the sugar. Spread half this mixture on a plate and arrange the herring fillets on top. Dust them with the remaining salt and sugar mixture and leave them to stand for 30 minutes.

**2** Prepare the marinade: chop the onions finely. Put them into a saucepan with the vinegar and the same amount of water. Add the remaining sugar, coriander seeds, cloves and pepper. Stir and bring to the boil over a low heat. Leave to simmer for 10 minutes, then leave to go cold.

**3** When the herring fillets have been standing for 30 minutes, rinse them and wipe dry. Arrange them in a casserole dish, in layers, spooning on the marinade as you work. Finally, coat the top with marinade and leave to stand in the refrigerator for at least 12 hours before serving. Serve the herrings with slices of rye bread and unsalted butter.

# Schol Uit de Oven

## Oven-baked White Fish Fillets

SERVES 4

*8 sole fillets, 75 g/3 oz each, skinned and boned*
*40 g/1½ oz melted butter*
*cayenne pepper to taste*
*40 g/1½ oz split almonds*
*65 g/2½ oz Gouda cheese, cut into small strips*
*8 thin rashers smoked bacon*
*salt and pepper*

**1** Preheat the oven to Gas Mark 8/230°C/450°F. Rinse the sole fillets and wipe dry. Make shallow parallel cuts on the undersides with the point of a sharp knife. Put the melted butter into an oven dish large enough to hold the fish in one layer. Coat the fillets in the melted butter. Season them with salt and pepper and dust them with cayenne pepper.

**2** Brown the almonds in a dry pan and set them aside in a bowl.

**3** Top the fish with the cheese and toasted almonds. Transfer the dish to the oven and leave to cook for 12 minutes until the Gouda starts to melt.

**4** While the fish is cooking, brown the bacon on both sides in a dry pan and keep it hot.

**5** Place a rasher of bacon on top of each fish fillet and serve hot from the oven dish.

# HUTSPOT

## *Dutch Hot-Pot*

SERVES 6-8

*1.5 kg/3½ lb rib of beef, off the bone*
*1 sprig thyme*
*1 bay leaf*
*2 cloves*
*1 small mace blade*
*1 tablespoon coarsely ground pepper*
*2 shallots or small onions*
*2 garlic cloves*
*500 g/1 lb potatoes, firm variety*
*4 carrots*
*500 g/1 lb celeriac*
*50 g/2 oz butter*

To serve:
*various types of mustard*
*coarse rock salt*

**1** Rinse and wipe dry the meat. Boil some water in a large casserole. Put in the meat and boil hard for 10 minutes. Then drain the meat and discard the water. Rinse the meat and the casserole.

**2** Put the meat back into the casserole and cover it with cold water. Put the thyme, bay leaf, cloves, mace and pepper into a muslin spice bag and tie it up. Add the whole shallots, whole garlic cloves and spice bag to the meat. Bring to the boil over a low heat and cover the casserole. Leave to simmer for 2½ hours.

**3** Thirty minutes before the end of the cooking time, prepare the vegetables: peel the potatoes, carrots and celeriac. Rinse them and wipe dry. Cut the carrots in half lengthwise and chop the celeriac into thick pieces. Leave the potatoes whole.

**4** When the meat is cooked, add the vegetables and cook for a further 30 minutes, still on a low heat and covered.

**5** Once the hot-pot is cooked, drain the vegetables and mash them with a fork, adding the butter and about 100 ml/3½ fl oz of the broth to make a smooth, very thick purée. Slice the meat.

**6** Arrange the meat on a serving dish and surround it with the vegetable purée. Serve hot, accompanied by a variety of mustards and the rock salt. The broth may be served as a soup first, as it is, or with pasta shells added. Beaten egg may be added through a sieve, so that thin threads of cooked egg form in it after 2 minutes' cooking.

# GEHAKTBALLEN

## *Meatballs*

SERVES 4

*100 ml/3½ fl oz milk*
*65 g/2½ oz white bread (without crusts)*
*6 pinches grated nutmeg*
*2 young onions*
*625 g/1¼ lb minced beef*
*2 tablespoons chopped flat-leaf parsley*
*2 tablespoons oil*
*salt and pepper*

**1** Boil the milk in a small saucepan, crumble in the bread and add salt, pepper and the nutmeg. Leave to boil up for 3 minutes, stirring with a wooden spatula until you have a smooth, thick consistency. Remove the saucepan from the heat and leave the sauce to go cold.

**2** Wash the onions and chop them finely. Put them into a large bowl with the mince, parsley and contents of the saucepan. Fold in the latter, first with the spatula and then with your hands until everything is thoroughly mixed together.

**3** Make walnut-sized meatballs from the mixture, rolling them between your palms. To facilitate this, wet your hands with cold water between each one.

**4** Heat the oil in a large non-stick frying pan. Cook the meatballs for 6 minutes on a medium heat, shaking the pan with a circular movement so they roll over and cook evenly without breaking. Serve them hot with a salad or green vegetables.

# NETHERLANDS

Erwtensoep
*(Split Pea Soup)*

Flensjes
*(Dutch Pancake Cake)*

Maatjesharing
*(Marinated Herrings)*

# FLENSJES

## *Dutch Pancake Cake*

The Dutch often fill their pancakes with stewed fruit, but this recipe gives a delicious filling of chocolate and almonds.

SERVES 8-10

For the pancakes:
*250 g/8 oz flour*
*2 eggs*
*1 tablespoon caster sugar*
*1 pinch salt*
*500 ml/18 fl oz milk*
*50 g/2 oz butter*

For the filling:
*125 g/4 oz plain chocolate*
*125 g/4 oz ground almonds*
*3 eggs*
*100 g/3½ oz caster sugar*
*500 ml/18 fl oz milk*
*125 ml/4 fl oz thick* crème fraîche

1  Prepare the pancake batter: sieve the flour into a bowl, make a well in the centre and break the eggs in. Add the sugar and salt and drizzle in the milk, stirring continuously, to obtain a smooth, thick consistency. Strain the batter into another bowl and leave it to stand for 1 hour.

2  At the end of this time, cook the pancakes: melt the butter in a small frying pan or crêpe pan approximately 20 cm/8 inches in diameter, and then pour the bulk of it out into a bowl. This butter will be used as you go along to lightly grease the pan between pancakes. Ladle some batter into the pan and allow it to spread out to the edges, tipping the pan slightly from side to side. Cook the pancake for 30 seconds, then turn it and cook the other side. Keep the pancake warm on a plate on top of a saucepan of boiling water. Repeat this method for each pancake: you will have enough batter for 20-25.

3  Grease a deep cake tin of the same size or slightly larger than the pancakes with the remaining melted butter. Grate the chocolate using a coarse grater.

4  Preheat the oven to Gas Mark 4/180°C/350°F. Place a pancake on the bottom of the tin and dust it with chocolate. Place a second on top and dust it with ground almonds. Continue in the same way until all the pancakes are used, and finish with a plain pancake. Beat the eggs with the sugar. Add the milk and cream and pour the mixture into the tin. Press down with a spatula so the cream makes its way between the pancakes. Cover the tin with a sheet of greased tinfoil and place it in a cold bain-marie or a large shallow pan such as a roasting tin filled with cold water to within 2.5 cm/1 inch of the top.

5  Transfer the cake to the oven and leave to cook for 1½ hours. During cooking remove the tinfoil from time to time and press down on the pancakes so the cake does not swell up too much. When it is cooked, remove it from the oven and leave it to cool. Refrigerate it for 12 hours before serving.

6  When you are ready to serve it, turn the cake out and cut it into wedges. Serve it with whipped cream.

# RIFTKOEKJES

## *Grated Potato Cakes*

These potato cakes go well with all kinds of meat and roast or fried poultry.

SERVES 3

*375 g/12 oz potatoes, floury variety*
*1 egg*
*1 tablespoon thick* crème fraîche
*3 tablespoons groundnut oil*
*salt and pepper*

1  Peel and grate the potatoes into a bowl, using a very coarse grater.

2  Break the egg into a bowl and beat it with a fork, incorporating the cream. Season with salt and pepper and pour this mixture over the potato. Mix well together.

3  Heat the oil in a large non-stick frying pan and spread the potato mixture over, making 6 separate little cakes. Cook the potato cakes for 6 minutes each side, then drain them on kitchen paper and serve them hot.

# KALFSSCHNITZEL

## *Stuffed Veal Escalopes*

SERVES 6

*150 g/5 oz cooked ham*
*50 g/2 oz walnuts*
*100 g/3½ oz Gouda cheese*
*1 tablespoon chopped flat-leaf parsley*
*6 pinches grated nutmeg*
*6 very thin veal escalopes, 125 g/4 oz each*
*6 thin slices Parma ham, 75 g/3 oz each*
*2 tablespoons groundnut oil*
*25 g/1 oz butter*
*salt and pepper*

**1** Prepare the filling: finely chop the cooked ham in a food processor or blender. Do the same with the walnuts. Grate the Gouda coarsely. Mix together the cooked ham, walnuts, Gouda, parsley, nutmeg, salt and pepper.

**2** Spread an escalope out on your work surface. Place a slice of Parma ham on top and add one-sixth of the filling. Fold the escalope in 3, enclosing the stuffing, and pin the edges together with wooden cocktail sticks. Do the same with the remaining escalopes.

**3** Heat the oil in a large frying pan. Put in half the butter and when it has melted, cook the escalopes for 8 minutes each side on a medium heat.

**4** When the escalopes are cooked, set them aside in a deep dish to keep warm. Remove the cooking fat and deglaze the pan with 2 tablespoons of water. Add the remaining butter, melt it over a very low heat and coat the escalopes with this sauce. Serve immediately with fresh pasta, potato cakes (page 88) or green vegetables.

# ERWTENSOEP

## *Split Pea Soup*

SERVES 6

*2 thick rashers unsmoked bacon, 150 g/5 oz each*
*1 smoked uncooked sausage*
*200 g/7 oz peeled celeriac flesh*
*500 g/1 lb split peas*
*salt and pepper*

**1** Boil some water in a large saucepan and drop in the bacon. Simmer for 30 minutes, then add the sausage, pricked a few times with a fork. Cook for a further 30 minutes, then drain the bacon and sausage.

**2** Cut the celeriac into 1 cm/½-inch cubes. Put the split peas into a large round cocotte and cover them with 1.5 litres/2½ pints of cold water. Add the celeriac and bacon and bring to the boil. Cover and leave to cook for 45 minutes on a reduced heat, stirring from time to time. Check that the peas have softened.

**3** Meanwhile, skin and slice the sausage. Set it aside between two plates so it does not dry up.

**4** When the peas are cooked, take out the bacon and cut it into 1 cm/½-inch thick strips. Put it back in the pot, on top of the split peas, with the slices of sausage. Leave to stand, covered, for 5 minutes.

**5** Divide the soup between 6 heated soup plates and serve immediately. Add pepper at the last minute. This soup may be garnished with croûtons.

# GREECE

*GREEK GASTRONOMY DATES BACK TO ANCIENT TIMES.*
*It was hymned by Homer and developed by Archastrates.*

The variety and quality of produce and the art of cooking and combining it have always been noteworthy. All the good things the sun produces have been found in this country blessed by the gods, since time immemorial. The ancient Greeks ate bread, game, lamb, olives and olive oil, honey, goat's and ewe's cheese, shellfish and fish, grapes, figs, almonds and berries. They knew the aromatic plants and herbs which have survived through the centuries: oregano, coriander, parsley, fennel, mint, cumin, garlic, pepper and shallots. They drank milk, mead and wine diluted with water.

Today the Greeks drink the wine of their generous vines; cook lamb (the main ingredient of the world-famous *moussaka*) better than ever and raise it in large numbers; eat citrus fruit, aubergines, peppers, courgettes and tomatoes, which they imported and which, since their introduction, have held an important place in Greek cuisine. Yogurt is used in everything: thick, velvety and oily, Greek yogurt is the best in the world. It can be eaten raw

or cooked, sweet or savoury: *tzatziki* and *tarato* are favourites with gourmets the world over. A great variety of Greek cheeses figure in every menu: the best known, fetta, is widely exported and used in many recipes. It is included in Greek salad - with tomatoes, cucumbers, peppers and Kalamata olives - in *tiropites* and *spanakopites*, pastries made of crisp leaves of filo pastry which is itself exported all over the world. All Graecophiles enjoy the ritual of eating *meze*, which may include diced vegetable omelette, pieces of hot cheese, lamb's brains in lemon sauce, squid in garlic vinaigrette, stuffed clams, fried squid, grilled prawns, spiced mussels, pickled peppers, aubergine salad, *keftedes* (meatballs), stuffed vine leaves, *taramasalata*, etc. They make the ideal accompaniment to an aperitif, a starter or even a whole meal. In cold countries, these recipes evoke the sun and inspire the desire to drink chilled ouzo or one of the inimitable resinous Greek wines. But such wines do not travel well and they are worth visiting Greece to drink.

# SOUPA RIZI AVGHOLEMONO

## *Lemon Soup with Egg and Rice*

SERVES 4

*1.5 litres/2½ pints chicken stock*
*6 tablespoons round-grain rice*
*4 tablespoons chopped flat-leaf parsley*
*2 egg yolks*
*4 tablespoons lemon juice*
*salt and pepper*

**1** Put the chicken stock into a saucepan and bring to the boil. Put the rice in and leave it to cook for about 18 minutes, until the rice is just tender.

**2** Add the parsley and cook the soup for a further 3 minutes. Season to taste.

**3** Meanwhile, beat the egg yolks and lemon juice together in a bowl. Beat in a ladleful of the soup.

**4** When the rice is cooked, pour the contents of the bowl into the saucepan, stirring continuously. Leave it to simmer for 3 minutes until the soup has thickened slightly, without allowing it to boil.

**5** Pour the soup into a tureen and serve immediately. Season with pepper at the table.

# TOMATOSOUPA ME FIDHES

## *Tomato Soup with Vermicelli*

SERVES 6

*1 kg/2 lb just ripe tomatoes*
*1 small carrot*
*1 celery stick, tender inner one with leaves*
*2 young onions*
*2 garlic cloves*
*2 tablespoons extra virgin olive oil*
*½ teaspoon caster sugar*
*1 litre/1¾ pints water*
*75 g/3 oz vermicelli*
*salt and pepper*

**1** Scald the tomatoes in boiling water for 10 seconds, cool them under cold running water, skin, halve and de-seed them. Roughly chop the flesh. Peel the carrot and rinse it, together with the celery. Finely chop the carrot, celery, onions and garlic.

**2** Heat the oil in a large round casserole. Put in the chopped vegetables and cook them for 3 minutes until they just start to turn golden, stirring continuously. Add the tomatoes, sugar, salt and pepper and stir for a further 2 minutes. Pour on the water, bring to the boil, cover the casserole and cook gently for 40 minutes.

**3** At the end of this time, put the soup through a blender and then pour it back into the rinsed casserole. Bring to the boil, add the vermicelli and leave to cook for 3-4 minutes until the noodles are just tender. Turn the soup into a tureen and serve immediately.

# TIROPITA STO TAPSI

## *Cheese Pastries*

SERVES 6

*200 g/7 oz unsalted fetta cheese*
*50 g/2 oz grated parmesan*
*4 pinches grated nutmeg*
*2 tablespoons chopped chives*
*1 unwaxed lemon*
*1 egg, beaten*
*12 squares filo pastry*
*1 teaspoon oil*
*salt and pepper*

**1** Preheat the oven to Gas Mark 6/200°C/400°F. Crush the fetta in a bowl with a fork. Add the parmesan, salt, pepper, nutmeg and chives. Wash the lemon and grate the zest into the bowl. Mix well together. Stir in the egg.

**2** Place 1 square of filo pastry on your work surface. Using one-twelfth of the cheese mixture, place a 6 cm/2½-inch rectangle of filling on the centre of the lower half. Fold over the pastry from the bottom end first, then fold over the sides and finally roll it up, tucking in the ends.

**3** Brush the bottom and sides of a 30 cm/12-inch gratin dish with oil. Arrange the filo rolls in this, at least 1 cm apart. Very lightly brush them with oil.

**4** Transfer the dish to the oven and cook the pastries for 15-20 minutes. Serve the crispy pastries hot or warm.

# GIGANTES PLAKI

## *Haricot Beans with Tomato*

The Greeks make this dish with huge white haricot beans. They go well with all roast meat dishes.

SERVES 6

*200 g/7 oz dried haricot beans*
*500 g/1 lb just ripe tomatoes*
*200 g/7 oz onions*
*2 tablespoons olive oil*
*1 bay leaf*
*1 sprig fresh savory*
*2 tablespoons chopped flat-leaf parsley*
*salt and pepper*

**1** To prepare the beans, first soak them in cold water for at least 8 hours. Then drain them and put them into a large saucepan. Cover them generously with cold salted water and leave to cook for 1 hour.

**2** Meanwhile, scald the tomatoes in boiling water for 10 seconds, cool them under cold running water, skin, halve and de-seed them; roughly chop the flesh. Finely chop the onions.

**3** Heat the oil in a large round casserole and cook the onions in this for 2 minutes until they have just turned golden, stirring continuously with a wooden spatula. Add the tomatoes, bay leaf, savory and parsley. Season with salt and pepper and stir. Leave to cook on a very low heat for 30 minutes.

**4** When the beans are cooked, drain them and put them into the tomato sauce. Leave to cook for a further 15 minutes, covered, stirring from time to time, until the beans are tender. Serve hot.

# KALAMARES YEMISTA

## *Stuffed Squid*

SERVES 4

*8 squid, 100 g/3½ oz each*
*25 g/1 oz pine kernels*
*50 g/2 oz cooked long-grain rice*
*50 g/2 oz sultanas*
*2 tablespoons chopped flat-leaf parsley*
*3 tablespoons olive oil*
*1 garlic clove*
*4 pinches ground cinnamon*
*4 pinches grated nutmeg*
*250 g/8 oz ripe tomatoes*
*1 teaspoon crushed oregano*
*salt and pepper*

1 Prepare the squid: put the first one flat on your work surface and hold the top in one hand. Take hold of the tentacles with the other hand and gently pull: discard innards and bone. Keep only the tentacles from the head part, cut at the level of the eyes; wash and wipe dry. Wash the inside of the squid; if there are eggs or soft roe, leave them - they are delicious. Remove the fine skin which covers the squid and wipe dry. Detach the fins and add them to the tentacle meat. Repeat for the remaining squid. Slice the fins and tentacles.

2 Brown the pine kernels in a non-stick, dry pan and set them aside in a bowl. Add the rice, sultanas and parsley.

3 Preheat the oven to Gas Mark 7/220°C/425°F. Heat half a tablespoon of the olive oil in a medium saucepan. Put in the sliced squid and cook on a low heat for 3 minutes. Add the nut mixture, salt, pepper, crushed garlic clove, cinnamon and nutmeg. Stir for 30 seconds. Sprinkle with a further half tablespoon of the oil, stir again and remove the pan from the heat. Leave to cool.

4 Stuff the squid bodies with this mixture, using wooden cocktail sticks to close them up. Rinse the stuffed squid under running water, holding them upright. Wipe dry.

5 Scald the tomatoes for 10 seconds in boiling water, cool them under cold running water, skin, halve and de-seed them; roughly chop the flesh. Put the remaining oil in a 30 cm/12-inch oven dish and add the tomato, salt, pepper and oregano. Mix well. Arrange the stuffed squid in the baking dish, turning them to coat them well with the aromatic oil. Transfer the dish to the oven and leave the squid to cook for 30 minutes. Half-way through cooking, baste them with the cooking juices and turn them over.

6 Take the squid out of the oven and serve them from the cooking dish. They may be served hot, warm or cold.

# GREECE

Arni Souvlaki
*(Lamb Kebabs with Lemon)*

Tiropita sto Tapsi
*(Cheese Pastries)*

Briami
*(Stuffed Vegetables)*

# KOTOPOULO LEMONATO

## *Roast Chicken with Lemon*

### SERVES 4

*1 chicken, 1.5 kg/3½ lb, jointed into 10 pieces*
*2 tablespoons olive oil*
*25 g/1 oz butter*
*1 teaspoon oregano*
*2 unwaxed lemons*
*salt and pepper*

**1** Skin the chicken pieces. Rinse them and wipe dry. Season with salt and pepper.

**2** Preheat the oven to Gas Mark 6/200°C/400°F. Heat the oil in a large frying pan. Add the butter and when it has melted, brown the chicken pieces on all sides for about 15 minutes. Arrange the chicken pieces in a 30 cm/12-inch oven dish.

**3** Put the oregano in a bowl. Wash and wipe dry the lemons; finely grate the zest into the bowl. Cut the lemons in half and squeeze the juice into the bowl too. Sprinkle the chicken pieces with this aromatic lemon mixture. Transfer the dish to the oven and leave the chicken to cook for about 1 hour, turning it once during cooking. If the juice evaporates too quickly, add a little water to the bottom of the baking dish.

**4** When the chicken is cooked, arrange it on a serving dish and serve immediately. It is also delicious served cold.

# KEFTEDHAKIA LEMONATA

## *Lamb Meatballs in Lemon Sauce*

### SERVES 4

*2 tablespoons long-grain rice*
*1 onion*
*1 tablespoon chopped flat-leaf parsley*
*1 egg white*
*500 g/1 lb minced lamb*
*500 ml/18 fl oz vegetable stock*
*20 g/¾ oz butter*
*2 egg yolks*
*2 tablespoons lemon juice*
*salt and pepper*

**1** Wash the rice and leave it to soak for 10 minutes in tepid water. Grate the onion into a large bowl, using the coarse side of a grater. Add the parsley, salt and pepper. Lightly beat the egg white with a fork, add it to the onion and mix well.

**2** Drain the rice and add it to the bowl, together with the mince. Work it together with your hands to make a smooth mixture. Cover the bowl and leave the mixture to chill in the refrigerator for 1 hour.

**3** At the end of this time, make walnut-sized meatballs from the mixture, rolling them between the palms of your hands. To facilitate this, wet your hands with cold water between each one. The mixture will make approximately 20 meatballs.

**4** Bring the vegetable stock to the boil in a large frying pan. Season with salt and add the butter. Drop in the meatballs. Bring the stock to the boil and reduce the heat. Simmer, uncovered, for 20 minutes, carefully stirring and turning the meatballs from time to time.

**5** When the meatballs are cooked, make the sauce. Whisk the egg yolks in a bowl with the lemon juice and 3 tablespoons of the cooking liquid from the meatballs. Pour this into the frying pan. Stir for 2 minutes without allowing the sauce to boil or even bubble - it must thicken over the lowest possible heat.

**6** Turn the meatballs and sauce out into a serving dish and serve immediately.

# ARNAKI ME KOUKIA

## *Lamb Stew with Broad Beans*

SERVES 6

*1.5 kg/3½ lb shoulder of lamb, boned out and
trimmed of fat
200 g/7 oz onions
250 g/8 oz tomatoes
2 garlic cloves
3 tablespoons olive oil
500 ml/18 fl oz water
1.5 kg/3½ lb fresh broad beans
3 tablespoons lemon juice
2 tablespoons chopped coriander leaves
salt and pepper*

**1** Cut the meat into 3 cm/1¼-inch cubes. Finely chop the onions. Scald the tomatoes in boiling water for 10 seconds, cool them under cold running water, skin, halve and de-seed them; chop the flesh. Cut the garlic cloves into quarters.

**2** Heat the oil in a large round casserole, put in the chopped onion and cook it for 3 minutes on a medium heat, turning frequently; add the meat, stir it in and brown it on all sides over a higher heat for 10 minutes. Add the garlic and tomato, mix well and season with salt and pepper.

**3** Pour the water into the casserole, cover it and leave the lamb to cook gently for 1½ hours on a low heat, stirring frequently.

**4** Meanwhile, shell the broad beans, removing the little top pieces.

**5** When the meat has been cooking for 1½ hours, put in the beans, lemon juice, salt and pepper. Stir, cover the casserole again and cook the stew for a further 30 minutes until the beans are really tender. Add the coriander, stir and serve immediately.

# ARNI SOUVLAKI

## *Lamb Kebabs with Lemon*

SERVES 6

*2 garlic cloves
1 unwaxed lemon
6 tablespoons olive oil
1 teaspoon oregano
2 bay leaves, fresh if possible
1.25 kg/3 lb shoulder of lamb, boned out and
trimmed of fat
salt and pepper*

**1** Crush the garlic and put it in a large bowl. Wash the lemon, wipe it dry and grate the zest into the bowl; cut the lemon in half, and squeeze the juice into the bowl. Add the oil, oregano and the bay leaves, lightly crushed in your fingers. Season with salt and pepper and mix well.

**2** Cut the meat into 3 cm/1¼-inch cubes and put them into the bowl. Mix well, cover the bowl and leave the meat to marinate for 12 hours in the refrigerator.

**3** When the meat has marinated, drain it and divide it between 6 long skewers.

**4** Preheat a meat grill and brush the kebabs lightly with oil. When the grill is hot, lay the kebabs on the surface and cook them briskly for 8-10 minutes, turning and basting them frequently using the marinade juices.

**5** When the kebabs are cooked, arrange them on a dish and serve immediately with grilled vegetables and lemon quarters.

# KEFTEDHES ME SALSA TOMATA

## *Meatballs in Tomato Sauce*

SERVES 6

*100 ml/3½ fl oz milk*
*50 g/2 oz white bread, crusts cut off*
*4 pinches grated nutmeg*
*1 unwaxed lemon*
*625 g/1¼ lb minced meat: mixture of beef, veal and lamb in equal quantities*
*2 tablespoons chopped flat-leaf parsley*
*salt and pepper*

For the tomato sauce:
*1 large onion*
*1 tablespoon olive oil*
*25 g/1 oz butter*
*200 ml/7 fl oz fresh tomato sauce (see spaghetti alla napoletana, page 34)*
*4 pinches oregano*
*salt and pepper*

**1** Prepare the meatballs: boil up the milk in a small saucepan, and crumble in the bread; add salt, pepper and the nutmeg. Boil the milk for 3 minutes, stirring with a wooden spatula, until you have a smooth, creamy paste. Take the pan off the heat and leave the sauce to go cold.

**2** Wash the lemon, wipe it dry and grate half the zest into a large bowl. Put in the minced meats, parsley and contents of the saucepan. Mix well, first with a spatula and then by hand until everything is thoroughly mixed together.

**3** Make walnut-sized meatballs from the mixture, rolling them between the palms of your hands. To facilitate this, wet your hands with cold water between each one. The mixture will make approximately 24 meatballs.

**4** Prepare the tomato sauce: finely chop the onion. Heat the oil in a large frying pan and add the butter. When the butter has melted, put in the onions and stir continuously for 3 minutes until they have just turned golden. Add the meatballs and fry them until they have turned golden. Pour in the tomato sauce and oregano, and season. Bring the sauce to

the boil, cover the pan and cook for 30 minutes on a low heat. Turn the meatballs frequently during cooking.

**5** When the meatballs are cooked, arrange them on a hot serving dish. If necessary, boil the sauce for a few minutes to reduce it to a thick consistency. Pour the sauce around the meatballs and serve them immediately.

# KOJOKIDHALIA GRATIN

## *Gratin of Courgettes*

SERVES 4

*500 g/1 lb courgettes*
*3 tablespoons olive oil*
*200 g/7 oz fetta cheese*
*3 eggs*
*50 g/2 oz parmesan, grated finely and freshly*
*3 tablespoons white breadcrumbs*
*salt and pepper*

**1** Preheat the oven to Gas Mark 6/200°C/400°F. Wash, wipe dry and finely grate the courgettes. Put them into a large frying pan with 2 tablespoons of the oil and 4 tablespoons of water. Leave the courgettes to cook for about 10 minutes, stirring frequently, until they are just tender.

**2** Crush the fetta finely in a bowl. Whisk the eggs in a separate bowl, and add the fetta and the parmesan. Season with salt and pepper.

**3** When the courgettes are cooked, add them to the egg and cheese mixture and mix well.

**4** Oil a 30 cm/12-inch gratin dish and pour in the mixture. Smooth the surface with a spatula and sprinkle with the breadcrumbs. Transfer the dish to the oven and cook the gratin for 45 minutes until it is golden on top. Serve it hot from the gratin dish.

# POLYPIKILLO

## *Baked Vegetables*

SERVES 4-5

*500 g/1 lb fresh onions*
*500 g/1 lb courgettes*
*2 aubergines*
*750 g/1½ lb ripe but firm tomatoes*
*2 garlic cloves*
*6 tablespoons olive oil*
*3 tablespoons brown breadcrumbs*
*salt and pepper*

**1** Cut the onions into 5 mm/¼-inch slices, including the tender green part. Wash the courgettes, aubergines and tomatoes and wipe them dry. Cut the aubergines and courgettes into oblique slices 5 mm/¼ inch thick. Slice the tomatoes as thinly as possible. Finely chop the garlic.

**2** Preheat the oven to Gas Mark 6/200°C/400°F. Heat 4 tablespoons of the oil in a 30 cm/12-inch gratin dish and cook the onions on a low heat for 8 minutes, turning them frequently, until they turn transparent. Add the garlic, salt and pepper, stir and cook gently for another 2 minutes.

**3** Remove the dish from the heat and smooth the onions over the base. Arrange the courgette, aubergine and tomato slices alternately in 4 lengthwise rows, on top of the onions. Sprinkle the vegetables with the breadcrumbs, moisten them with the remaining oil and season with salt and pepper.

**4** Transfer the dish to the oven and leave the vegetables to cook for 45 minutes. Serve them hot or warm from the gratin dish.

# KOUKIA ME ANGUINARES

## *Casserole of Artichokes and Broad Beans*

This combination of vegetables goes well with lamb, any roast white meat or fish fillets.

SERVES 4

*1.5 kg/3½ lb fresh broad beans*
*2 young onions*
*6 medium-size globe artichokes*
*½ lemon*
*2 tablespoons olive oil*
*2 tablespoons chopped coriander leaves*
*salt*

**1** Shell the beans and remove the tender green casing. Finely chop the onions.

**2** Prepare the artichokes: cut off the stem close to the bottom of the heart and remove the tough outer leaves. Cut the tender leaves 5 mm/¼ inch from the heart. Trim the hearts and rub them with the cut lemon half. Cut each heart into quarters and remove the hard core. Cut each quarter into 2 strips.

**3** Heat the oil in a large round casserole. Put in the onions and cook them gently for 2 minutes, stirring with a wooden spatula, without allowing them to turn golden. Add the artichoke pieces and cook them for 7-8 minutes on a moderate heat, stirring continuously: the artichokes should be lightly golden and almost tender.

**4** Add 3 tablespoons of water to the casserole and put in the beans and coriander. Season with salt. Mix well. Cover the casserole and cook the beans for 7 minutes. Remove the casserole from the heat and serve immediately.

# BRIAMI

## Stuffed Vegetables

SERVES 4

*2 green peppers, 100 g/3½ oz each*
*1 aubergine, 250 g/8 oz*
*2 fat courgettes, 75 g/3 oz each*
*2 onions, 75 g/3 oz each*

For the filling:
*300 g/10 oz lean minced beef*
*50 g/2 oz cooked long-grain rice*
*1 egg*
*1 small garlic clove*
*1 tablespoon chopped mint*
*1 tablespoon chopped flat-leaf parsley*
*grated zest of 1 unwaxed lemon*
*4 tablespoons olive oil*
*1 large tomato*
*1 sprig thyme*
*salt and pepper*

**1** Rinse the vegetables and wipe them dry. Cut the peppers in half across their width and remove the seeds and cores. Cut the aubergine in half vertically and remove the stalk; do the same with the courgettes. Cut the onions in half horizontally. Scrape the middle out of the aubergine, courgettes and onions to within 1 cm of the skin. Chop the flesh of each of these vegetables separately.

**2** Preheat the oven to Gas Mark 6/200°C/400°F. Prepare the stuffing: put the meat into a bowl with the rice and the egg. Crush the garlic and add it to the bowl. Add the mint, parsley, zest of lemon, salt and pepper and mix well.

**3** Heat 2 tablespoons of the oil in a large non-stick frying pan and brown the chopped onion slightly in this. Add the chopped aubergine, stir for 3 minutes, then add the chopped courgette and stir for a further 3 minutes. Turn the vegetables out into the bowl with the meat mixture and mix well. Scald the tomato in boiling water for 10 seconds, cool it under cold running water, skin, halve and de-seed it; roughly chop the flesh. Add it to the bowl and mix again.

**4** Divide the stuffing between the vegetable halves and arrange them in a large, lightly oiled gratin dish. Put 3 tablespoons of water in the bottom of

the dish and sprinkle the vegetables with the remaining oil. Sprinkle them with thyme and transfer the dish to the oven. Cook the vegetables for about 1 hour, until they are tender and the stuffing is golden brown. Baste them often during cooking.

**5** When the vegetables are cooked, arrange them on a plate. Serve them hot, warm or cold.

# GLYMISMA AMIGTHALOU

## Almond Cakes

SERVES 6-8

*250 g/8 oz plain flour*
*1 teaspoon baking powder*
*75 g/3 oz butter*
*50 g/2 oz caster sugar*
*3 eggs*
*125 ml/4 fl oz whole milk yogurt*
*150 g/5 oz ground almonds*

For the sugar syrup:
*200 g/7 oz sugar*
*2 tablespoons lemon juice*
*3 tablespoons water*

To decorate:
*blanched almonds*

**1** Preheat the oven to Gas Mark 4/180°C/350°F. Butter a 28 cm/11-inch gratin dish. Sieve the flour and baking powder together.

**2** Cream the butter and sugar in a bowl, until the mixture is smooth. Incorporate the eggs, one by one, beating continuously. Add the yogurt, then the flour and baking powder mixture and the ground almonds. Mix one last time.

**3** Turn the mixture into the gratin dish, smooth the surface and transfer the dish to the oven. Leave the cake to cook for 20 minutes.

**4** Take the cake out of the oven and, using the point of a knife, mark out a pattern of diamond shapes on the surface, 1 cm/½ inch deep and 4 cm/1½ inches across. Put the cake back into the oven and leave it to cook for a further 10 minutes.

**5** Meanwhile, prepare the sugar syrup: put the sugar and lemon juice into a small saucepan. Add the water and bring to the boil. Allow it to boil up for 2 minutes, then remove the syrup from the heat and leave it to cool slightly.

**6** When the cake is cooked, take it out of the oven and run the knife over the diamond shapes again to cut them through completely. Pour the warm sugar syrup over the cake and leave it to go completely cold.

**7** When you are ready to serve the cake, cut out the diamond shapes and arrange them on a serving dish with an almond on top of each.

# BAKLAVA

## *Nut Pastries*

SERVES 8

*100 g/3½ oz butter*
*300 g/10 oz shelled mixed nuts*
*100 g/3½ oz shelled almonds*
*200 g/7 oz caster sugar, plus a little extra*
*1 teaspoon ground cinnamon*
*400 g/13 oz filo pastry*

For the sugar syrup:
*200 g/7 oz sugar*
*3 tablespoons water*
*4 tablespoons lemon juice*

**1** Preheat the oven to Gas Mark 6/200°C/400°F. Melt the butter and leave it to cool slightly. Put the mixed nuts and almonds into a blender or food processor and add the sugar and cinnamon. Process to a rough semolina consistency.

**2** Brush the bottom and sides of a 30 cm/12-inch gratin dish with melted butter. Spread 1 sheet of filo pastry on this, brush it with butter and sprinkle it with a little sugar. Put 3 more buttered and sugared sheets of pastry on top, keeping all the pastry edges inside the dish. Put half the nut mixture on this, spreading it out well with a spatula. Lay 3 more sheets of buttered and sugared filo pastry on top. Spread with the remaining nut mixture and lay the last sheets of pastry on this, buttered and sugared as before. Mark out 4 to 5 cm/1½ to 2-inch squares over the top, using the point of a small knife.

**3** Transfer the dish to the oven and leave the baklava to cook for about 45 minutes until the pastry turns golden.

**4** Make the sugar syrup: put the sugar into a small saucepan. Add the water and lemon juice. Bring to the boil and allow to boil up for 2 minutes.

**5** When the baklava is cooked, take it out of the oven and while it's still hot, pour over the boiling sugar syrup. Leave it to cool in the dish before cutting it into squares along the marked lines. Serve at room temperature.

# UNITED KINGDOM

## *FROM ENGLAND'S ROLLING GENTLENESS*
### *to the rugged Highlands of Scotland, from the warmer climes of the south to the*

cold and the gales of the north, the United Kingdom can be viewed as individual countries and as a whole. Its cuisine, which has been evolving since the Middle Ages, like that of other European countries, has been shaped by its climate and its history, most notably the exploration of the New World and the acquisition of its empire. Important contributions to international gastronomy such as roast beef, steak, sandwiches, afternoon tea, breakfast, and the invention of whisky and gin are evidence of the UK's gastronomic strength.

The British are proud of their national puddings, pies, cakes and jellies. Puddings and pies are the foundation of numerous British recipes. At first, the word 'pudding' simply meant anything boiled and later on came to mean any food steamed or simmered in a basin-shaped dish. Sweet and savoury, there are thousands of kinds of pudding, the most famous of which is probably Christmas pud-

ding: a rich, dried fruit pudding which is made months before it is to be eaten so as to give the flavour time to mature. When the pudding is brought to the table, brandy or rum is poured over it and set alight. The hot pudding is then served with brandy butter.

Like puddings, pies may be sweet or savoury. They are cooked in oval pie dishes which have a flat wide rim to hold the shortcrust or puff pastry or the mashed potato topping of, for example, a shepherd's pie, filled with succulent minced lamb and onion.

Cakes are eaten with afternoon tea, as are scones, crumpets and muffins – the last two served hot with butter and jam – and the famous little cucumber, cress, prawn, egg, smoked salmon or ham sandwiches. Tea is drunk too at breakfast time with the famous English breakfast of fried or scrambled eggs with sausages and bacon, fried tomatoes, kippers, porridge, cereal, buttered toast, jam and marmalade. Cold milk is always used for tea and is poured into the cup first, before the hot tea.

Cheese has always played a leading role: the Romans introduced and refined cheese-making techniques. Cheddar cheese – now world famous – has been produced since the seventeenth century; Cheshire, Wensleydale and Double Gloucester, Caerphilly and Stilton are almost as well known. The extensive coastal waters of the UK also yield their harvest – herring, mackerel, sole, oysters and other shellfish are plentiful and delicious.

Tea, so dear to the British heart, first came from China in the seventeenth century, before the colonisation of India which left such a heritage to Britain, not just of Indian tea which became the symbolic British drink, but also curry, basmati rice and chutneys. Indian restaurants have of course sprung up all over the country.

These historic trading links have opened up a formerly conservative country, which today offers an original, almost exotic, attractive range of cuisine which has that indefinable quality of charm which comes from being British.

# POTTED CRAB

SERVES 4

*1 large cooked female crab, 1.25 kg/3 lb*
*100 g/3½ oz butter, softened*
*zest of 1 unwaxed lemon*
*2 tablespoons lemon juice*
*6 pinches paprika*
*4 pinches chilli powder*
*6 pinches grated nutmeg*
*salt and pepper*

1 Remove the crab meat from the shell. Put all the white meat, including the claw meat, into a blender or food processor bowl. Add the butter, zest and juice of lemon, paprika, chilli powder, nutmeg, salt and pepper. Blend to a fine and smooth mixture.

2 Crumble the coral and creamy parts of the crab and stir them into the contents of the blender bowl. Set the mixture aside in a bowl in the refrigerator until ready to serve. Serve with slices of toast, sliced radishes, sliced cucumber, etc.

# MULLIGATAWNY SOUP

SERVES 6

*1 large onion*
*1 large carrot*
*1 large cooking apple*
*2 tablespoons oil*
*500 g/1 lb lean mutton or lamb, on the bone (chops ideal), well trimmed*
*2 teaspoons medium strength curry powder*
*1 teaspoon medium strength curry paste*
*1 litre/1¾ pints vegetable or chicken stock or water*
*1 teaspoon arrowroot*
*salt*

1 Finely chop the onion. Peel the carrot and cut it into small cubes. Peel and core the apple and cut it into small cubes.

2 Heat the oil in a cocotte. Brown the pieces of meat in this. Add the onion and carrot and continue cooking until these begin to turn golden. Then drain off the cooking oil.

3 Add the apple, with the curry powder and paste, and stir for 3 minutes.

4 Gradually add the stock or water, stirring well, and season with a little salt.

5 Cover and simmer the soup very slowly for 1½ to 2 hours, or until the meat is very tender.

6 Remove the meat and when it has cooled slightly, strip the meat from the bones. Return the meat to the soup and liquidise it all in a blender.

7 Return the soup to the rinsed cocotte and thicken it with the arrowroot blended with 1 tablespoon of cold water.

8 Serve the soup piping hot with a side dish of finely chopped raw green or yellow peppers and a little freshly chopped coriander.

# CELERY AND STILTON SOUP

This soup may also be served as follows: spread a few croûtons with Stilton and place them in the bottom of each soup bowl; pour the soup over.

SERVES 6

*1 head of celery*
*1 onion*
*50 g/2 oz butter*
*½ teaspoon arrowroot*
*125 ml/4 fl oz dry white wine*
*1 litre/1 ¾ pints chicken stock*
*100 g/3½ oz Stilton*
*2 tablespoons double cream*
*salt and pepper*

**1** Finely chop the celery, reserving the young leaves for the garnish. Finely chop the onion.

**2** Melt the butter in a large round cocotte and put in the celery and onion. Stir for 5 minutes over a medium heat until the vegetables have turned golden. Dilute the arrowroot in the wine.

**3** Add the wine and chicken stock to the cocotte. Season with salt and pepper, cover and leave to simmer for 45 minutes, or until the celery is really tender.

**4** Leave the soup to cool slightly, then purée it in a liquidiser or push it through a wire sieve. Return the soup to the rinsed cocotte and heat it through gently.

**5** Crumble the Stilton and stir it into the soup with the cream. Do not allow it to boil after these have been added.

**6** Pour the soup into a tureen, garnish it with the celery leaves and serve immediately.

# TROUT IN CIDER

SERVES 4

*4 trout, 150 g/5 oz each*
*4 shallots*
*2 tablespoons chopped flat-leaf parsley*
*50 g/2 oz butter*
*300 ml/½ pint dry cider*
*6 pinches grated nutmeg*
*salt and pepper*

**1** Ask the fishmonger to gut and clean the fish. Rinse them and wipe dry. Season with salt and pepper. Finely chop the shallots; mix the shallots and parsley together.

**2** Preheat the oven to Gas Mark 7/220°C/425°F. Using half the butter, grease a 30 cm/12-inch baking dish. Spread half the shallot and parsley mixture on the bottom; arrange the fish on top and sprinkle with the remaining shallot and parsley.

**3** Pour in the cider. Add salt, pepper and the nutmeg and dot with the remaining butter. Transfer the dish to the oven. Leave to cook for 30 minutes. Serve hot from the baking dish.

# PAN-FRIED DOVER SOLE

SERVES 4

*4 Dover sole, 300–375 g/10–12 oz each*
*2 tablespoons flour*
*150 g/5 oz butter*
*1 tablespoon lemon juice*
*salt and pepper*

**1** Ask the fishmonger to gut and clean the fish and remove the black skin. Rinse them and wipe dry. Season with salt and pepper. Dip the fish lightly in the flour and shake them to remove any excess.

**2** Using 2 frying pans, melt one-quarter of the butter in each and fry the sole in these for 4 minutes, skin side up, then turn them and cook them for a further 3 minutes. Set them aside to keep hot on 4 plates.

**3** Wipe out one of the pans and put in the remaining butter. Add the lemon juice and melt the butter over a very low heat. Coat the fish with this sauce and serve immediately.

# YORKSHIRE PUDDING

SERVES 6

*250 g/8 oz plain flour*
*3 eggs*
*400 ml/14 fl oz milk*
*1 teaspoon salt*
*3 tablespoons beef dripping*

**1** Put the flour into a blender or food processor bowl. Add the eggs, milk and salt and mix to a smooth batter which should be the consistency of thick cream. Leave it to stand in the refrigerator for 1 hour.

**2** At the end of this time, preheat the oven to Gas Mark 7/220°C/425°F. Put the beef dripping in a 30 cm/12-inch gratin dish, and put it in the oven for 2–3 minutes until the fat is just smoking. Pour in the pudding mixture and put the dish back in the oven. Leave to cook for 15 minutes without opening the oven door, then lower the heat to Gas Mark 6/200°C/400°F and cook for a further 15 minutes until the pudding has risen and turned golden. Serve it hot from the gratin dish, cut into wedges.

# TRADITIONAL ROAST BEEF WITH GRAVY

Traditionally served with Yorkshire pudding (left).

SERVES 6

*1 piece sirloin beef, 2 kg/4½ lb, boned and rolled*
*600 ml/1 pint wine, water or beef or vegetable stock*
*salt and pepper*

**1** Ask the butcher to tie the sirloin with string.

**2** Preheat the oven to Gas Mark 9/240°C/475°F. Lay the beef, fat side up, on a wire rack in a baking dish. When the oven is hot, put the meat in and leave it to cook for 15 minutes. At the end of this time reduce the heat to Gas Mark 6/200°C/400°F and cook the meat for a further 40 minutes to 1 hour depending on whether you like it rare, medium or well done.

**3** When the roast beef is cooked, turn off the heat and leave it to stand in the oven for 15 minutes before serving. Carve it in thick slices at the table.

**4** To make the gravy, pour off the excess fat from the baking dish. Deglaze the dish over a low heat with a little of the wine, water or stock, then add the rest of the liquid. Season the gravy with salt and pepper, bring it to the boil, and leave it to cook until it has reduced to the required consistency. Then strain it into a sauce-boat and serve it with the beef.

# GREAT BRITAIN

Traditional Roast
Beef

Yorkshire Pudding

# LANCASHIRE HOT-POT

SERVES 4

*8 small lamb chops*
*4 lamb's kidneys*
*1 kg/2 lb potatoes, firm variety*
*250 g/8 oz onions*
*25 g/1 oz cooking fat*
*500 ml/18 fl oz hot beef stock*
*salt and pepper*

**1** Ask the butcher to trim any excess fat from the chops and trim and quarter the kidneys. Season the chops and kidneys with salt and pepper.

**2** Peel and slice the potatoes into slices 5 mm/ ¼ inch thick. Finely chop the onions.

**3** Preheat the oven to Gas Mark 2/150°C/300°F. Heat the cooking fat in a large round casserole and brown the chops in this on both sides. Set them aside and brown the kidneys in the same way.

**4** Pour off the fat and arrange one-third of the potatoes on the bottom of the pot. Put a layer of half the chops, kidneys and onions on top. Arrange a second layer of potatoes on these, followed by the remaining chops, kidneys and onions and finishing with the last layer of potato. Pour over the hot stock, cover the casserole and transfer it to the oven. Leave to cook undisturbed for 2–2½ hours. Check that the meat is tender.

**5** At the end of the cooking time, remove the lid and put the hot-pot back into the oven. Leave it to cook until the stock has evaporated and the potatoes are crisp and golden, about 30 minutes. Serve hot from the casserole.

# STEAK AND KIDNEY PUDDING

One of the oldest British dishes, served hot from its pudding basin. Traditionally the basin is tied up with a freshly starched, attractively knotted cloth.

SERVES 4

For the suet crust pastry:
*250 g/8 oz self-raising flour*
*½ teaspoon salt*
*2 pinches pepper*
*125 g/4 oz shredded suet*
*8–9 tablespoons cold water*

For the filling:
*500 g/1 lb braising steak*
*100 g/3½ oz lamb's kidneys*
*2 tablespoons plain flour*
*1 onion*
*1 bay leaf*
*1 tablespoon dry sherry*
*3 tablespoons water*
*salt and pepper*

**1** First make the suet crust pastry: sieve the flour, salt and pepper together in a bowl. Stir in the suet and mix with just enough water to make a soft, but not wet, dough.

**2** Divide the dough into two pieces, three-quarters to line the basin and the remainder to make the lid of the pudding. Grease a 900 ml/1½-pint pudding basin with butter. Roll out the larger piece of dough and line it into the bottom and sides of the basin so it slightly overhangs the edge.

**3** Prepare the filling: cut the steak and kidney into 1 cm/½-inch cubes. Put the flour into a bowl and add salt and pepper. Roll the steak and kidney in the seasoned flour.

**4** Finely chop the onion. Mix it with the floured steak and kidney and fill the pudding with this mixture. Add the bay leaf, sherry and water. Roll out the remaining dough and place it on top of the pudding, pressing down well so that the two edges of dough stick well together. Trim the excess with a knife. Place a large piece of buttered greaseproof paper on top of the pudding, fold the edges round the basin and tie securely with string.

**5** Half fill the base of a steamer with water and bring to the boil. Put the prepared pudding into the perforated steamer and cover with the lid. Steam steadily for 4 hours, adding more boiling water to the base of the steamer, as required.

**6** When the pudding is cooked, bring it to the table in its basin, turn it out on to a serving plate and serve hot.

# GAME PIE

SERVES 6

*1 pheasant, dressed and ready to cook*
*750 g/1½ lb haunch of venison*
*2 leg portions of rabbit*
*1 large onion*
*2 tablespoons groundnut oil*
*50 g/2 oz butter*
*1 tablespoon flour*
*150 ml/¼ pint Madeira*
*500 ml/18 fl oz chicken stock*
*1 tablespoon chopped flat-leaf parsley*
*200 g/7 oz flaky pastry*
*1 egg yolk*
*salt and pepper*

**1** Cut the pheasant into 8 pieces. Cut the haunch of venison into 2 cm/¾-inch cubes. Chop the rabbit legs in half. Finely chop the onion.

**2** Heat the oil in a large round casserole and add half the butter. When it has melted, brown the meat on all sides, turning it with a wooden spatula and seasoning with salt and pepper as it cooks. Take the meat out and set it aside on a plate. Wipe out the pot and put in the remaining butter and the onion. Stir continuously until the onion is just golden. Add the flour and stir until it turns golden. Pour in the Madeira and allow half of it to evaporate. Put the meat back in with the stock and parsley. Bring it to the boil, then reduce the heat and leave to cook, covered, for 2 hours.

**3** At the end of 2 hours take the meat out of the pot and leave it to go cold. Boil up the cooking juices to reduce them to 200 ml/7 fl oz. Reserve.

**4** Preheat the oven to Gas Mark 7/220°C/425°F. Cut the pheasant and rabbit into 2 cm/¾-inch pieces, discarding any bones. Put all the meat into a 28 cm/11-inch gratin dish. Coat with the reduced cooking juices.

**5** Roll out the flaky pastry, 5 mm/¼ inch thick. Cut a strip of pastry 2 cm/¾ inch wide and long enough to encircle the top edge of the gratin dish. Press this into place and dampen it with a little beaten egg yolk. Place the remaining piece of pastry as a lid on top of the dish and seal the two edges well. Make 3 holes in the top and surround these with pastry leaves cut from the trimmings. Brush the top with the egg yolk to glaze.

**6** Transfer the pie to the oven and leave it to cook for 25-30 minutes until the pastry is golden. Serve it hot from the pie dish.

# KEDGEREE

Originating in India, this recipe has become a British favourite. Traditionally served as a breakfast dish since the mid-eighteenth century, it has now become a dish for any meal at any time of day.

SERVES 4

*1 litre/1¾ pints milk*
*500 g/1 lb smoked haddock fillets*
*100 g/3½ oz butter*
*200 g/7 oz long-grain rice*
*2 hard-boiled eggs*
*2 teaspoons curry powder*
*1 tablespoon chopped flat-leaf parsley*

**1** Pour the milk into a large saucepan or cocotte and put in the haddock fillets. Place the pan on a low heat and bring to the boil. Cover and leave to simmer gently for 5 minutes.

**2** Take out the fish with a slotted spatula and strain the milk into another saucepan. Bring to the boil. Add 25 g/1 oz of the butter and the rice. Leave to cook for about 18 minutes, stirring frequently, until the rice is tender. Drain well.

**3** Meanwhile, flake the haddock, removing the skin and any bones. Shell the eggs; dice the whites and sieve the yolks into a bowl. Reserve.

**4** Melt the remaining butter in a clean pan. Add the curry powder and stir for 2 minutes. Add the cooked rice and stir for 2–3 minutes until it is coated in the curry and butter mixture. Carefully stir in the haddock and diced white of egg.

**5** Remove the pan from the heat and add the parsley. Mix well and turn the kedgeree into a deep serving dish. Garnish with the sieved egg yolk and serve immediately.

# ROAST GOOSE WITH APPLE AND PRUNE STUFFING

SERVES 8

*100 g/3½ oz prunes*
*500 g/1 lb cooking apples*
*150 g/5 oz white bread, with crusts cut off*
*50 g/2 oz brown sugar*
*200 ml/7 fl oz chicken stock*
*4 kg/9 lb goose, ready to cook*
*500 ml/18 fl oz dry cider*
*2 tablespoons redcurrant jelly*
*salt and pepper*

**1** Soak the prunes in a bowl full of water for 8 hours in advance. Cold tea may also be used for this.

**2** Make the stuffing: drain, stone and roughly chop the prunes. Cut the apples into quarters, peel, core and roughly chop them. Put the bread through a food processor to make breadcrumbs and place this in a bowl with the prunes, apples, sugar and stock. Season with salt and pepper and mix well.

**3** Season the goose inside and out. Stuff the bird and sew up the openings with cotton.

**4** Preheat the oven to Gas Mark 6/200°C/400°F. Place the goose on a wire rack in a large rectangular oven dish and transfer it to the oven. Leave to cook for 45 minutes until the goose is browned. Pour off the fat from the dish, reduce the heat to Gas Mark 4/180°C/350°F and leave the goose to cook for a further 2½ hours, basting it regularly with the cider.

**5** When the goose is cooked, leave it to stand for at least 15 minutes in the oven with the heat turned off and the door partly open. Take the goose out of the oven and place it on a meat dish. Pour the cooking juices into a saucepan and remove the fat by skimming with a spoon or kitchen paper as it comes to the surface. Boil rapidly to reduce the juice to a syrupy consistency. Add the redcurrant jelly and allow this to melt before stirring the sauce and pouring it into a sauce-boat. Serve the goose with the sauce handed round separately. Accompany the dish with green vegetables and boiled potatoes.

# POTTED CHICKEN LIVERS

## SERVES 6

*500 g/1 lb chicken livers*
*125 g/4 oz butter*
*1 garlic clove*
*1 sprig thyme*
*1 tablespoon brandy*
*2 tablespoons port*
*salt and pepper*

**1** Trim, rinse and wipe dry the chicken livers.

**2** Melt half the butter in a large frying pan. Put in the chicken livers and crushed garlic and the sprig of thyme. Cook for 10 minutes on a low heat, stirring frequently. Season with salt and pepper.

**3** Take out the thyme and stir the livers so they break up into a mousse. Add the brandy and port. Put the mixture through a fine sieve and transfer it to a small round gratin dish, levelling the top. Melt the remaining butter in a saucepan and pour it over the mousse. Chill in the refrigerator until ready to serve. Cut it into wedges and serve with hot toast and butter.

# ELIZABETHAN PORK STEW

## SERVES 6

*1 piece pork shoulder, 1.25 kg/3 lb*
*250 g/8 oz onions*
*2 tablespoons groundnut oil*
*500 g/1 lb cooking apples*
*1 celery heart*
*100 g/3½ oz raisins*
*1 strip zest of orange*
*5 chopped sage leaves*
*2 tablespoons chopped flat-leaf parsley*
*250 ml/8 fl oz dry sherry*
*salt and pepper*

**1** Rinse and wipe dry the meat. Season it with salt and pepper. Finely chop the onions. Heat the oil in a large round cocotte and brown the meat on all sides. Set it aside on a plate and put the onions into the cocotte. Fry them until lightly golden, stirring continuously.

**2** Preheat the oven to Gas Mark 3/160°C/325°F. Cut the apples into quarters, and peel and core them. Cut the celery into fine slices. Mix the apple, celery, raisins, zest of orange, sage and parsley together.

**3** Place the meat on the bed of onions and surround it with the above mixture. Add the sherry and just enough water to cover the meat. Put on the lid and transfer the cocotte to the oven. Leave to cook, undisturbed, for 3 hours.

**4** At the end of this time remove the cocotte from the oven. Slice the meat and arrange it on a plate. Surround it with the apples, raisins and onions.

# SHEPHERD'S PIE

This dish can also be prepared using leftover cooked lamb or beef. If leftovers are used, there is no need to cook the meat before mixing it with the lightly browned onions.

SERVES 6

*750 g/1½ lb floury potatoes*
*125 g/4 oz onion*
*2 tablespoons groundnut oil*
*750 g/1½ lb trimmed and boned lamb, minced*
*1 tablespoon flour*
*150 ml/¼ pint beef stock*
*2 tablespoons chopped flat-leaf parsley*
*75 g/3 oz butter*
*a little milk*
*salt and pepper*

**1** Wash the potatoes and place in a saucepan. Cover with cold water and bring to the boil. Add salt and leave to cook for about 20 minutes until the tip of a knife can easily be inserted into the potatoes.

**2** Meanwhile peel and chop the onion. Heat the oil in a medium-size frying pan and fry the onion until soft, turning it with a spatula. Add the meat and brown it, stirring constantly. Add the flour and mix for 1 minute. Season with salt and pepper and pour in the stock. Cook for 2 minutes while continuing to stir. Add the parsley, mix and remove from the heat.

**3** Preheat the oven to Gas Mark 5/190°C/375°F. Grease an oval gratin dish 32 cm/13 inches long with a knob of butter and spread out the meat in it.

**4** Drain, peel and mash the potatoes. Incorporate the rest of the butter and the milk, season with salt and pepper and spread the mashed potato over the meat. Use a fork to make furrows on the surface of the mashed potato.

**5** Transfer the dish to the oven and bake for about 45 minutes until the potato topping is golden brown. Serve the shepherd's pie hot in the dish in which it was baked.

# GINGERBREAD CAKE

Ginger-flavoured cakes have been popular in England since the Middle Ages and gingerbread in a large variety of shapes was always sold at country fairs. Originally the texture was firm, almost a biscuit, but more recently the softer, stickier gingerbread cake has become more popular.

SERVES 8

*125 g/4 oz lard*
*175 g/6 oz soft brown sugar*
*3 tablespoons golden syrup*
*3 tablespoons treacle*
*2 teaspoons bicarbonate of soda*
*3 eggs*
*100 ml/3½ fl oz milk*
*350 g/12 oz plain flour*
*1 tablespoon ground ginger*
*2 teaspoons ground cinnamon*
*½ teaspoon salt*

**1** Preheat the oven to Gas Mark 2/150°C/300°F. Line a 30 x 20 cm/12 x 8-inch oven dish with a piece of greaseproof paper.

**2** Melt the lard in a saucepan. Add the sugar, golden syrup, treacle and bicarbonate of soda. Stir over a low heat until the sugar has melted. Remove the pan from the heat.

**3** Beat the eggs with the milk. Pour this into the saucepan and mix well.

**4** Sieve the flour, ginger, cinnamon and salt into a bowl. Stir in the contents of the saucepan, using a spatula.

**5** Turn this batter out into the lined dish and transfer it to the oven. Leave to cook for 50–55 minutes until the cake is well risen and springy to the touch. Leave to stand for 15 minutes before turning it out on to a wire rack to cool. Cover with a clean tea towel whilst cooling. Leave the cake for 12 hours before eating. Once baked, the sticky texture of this cake is greatly improved if it is stored for a few days in an airtight container.

# BUTTERMILK SCONES

Buttermilk is a traditional ingredient used in scones to enhance the flavour and give them a rich, light and slightly crumbly texture. Scones are delicious with clotted cream and home-made strawberry jam.

## MAKES APPROXIMATELY 10 SCONES

*200 g/8 oz self-raising flour*
*½ teaspoon salt*
*1 teaspoon baking powder*
*50 g/2 oz block margarine*
*2 teaspoons caster sugar*
*150 ml/¼ pint milk or buttermilk*

**1** Preheat the oven to Gas Mark 8/230°C/450°F. Butter a baking sheet.

**2** Sieve the flour, salt and baking powder into a bowl. Add the margarine and rub it into the flour, until the mixture resembles fine breadcrumbs.

**3** Stir in the sugar and milk. Using a knife, work the dough into a ball. It should be soft but not sticky.

**4** Roll the dough out to 2.5 cm/1 inch thick on a well floured surface. Using a pastry cutter, cut it into circles 5 cm/2 inches in diameter. Arrange the circles on the greased baking sheet and transfer it to the oven. Leave the scones to cook for 8–10 minutes, by which time they will be well risen and golden brown.

# APPLE PIE

SERVES 6

For the pastry:
*200 g/7 oz plain flour*
*2 pinches salt*
*65 g/2½ oz caster sugar*
*100 g/3½ oz unsalted butter*

For the filling:
*2 lb cooking apples*
*65 g/2½ oz caster sugar*
*½ teaspoon ground cinnamon*
*½ teaspoon vanilla essence*
*4 pinches grated nutmeg*

**1** Make the pastry: sieve the flour and salt into a bowl and add the sugar. Put in the butter and rub it in with your fingertips until it resembles fine breadcrumbs. Sprinkle in a little cold water and work the dough into a ball using a knife. It should be soft but not sticky. Wrap it in clingfilm and leave to stand in the refrigerator for 30 minutes.

**2** At the end of this time take the dough out of the refrigerator. Cut the apples into quarters; peel and core them. Slice them thickly. Put them into a bowl with the sugar, cinnamon, vanilla and nutmeg. Mix well.

**3** Preheat the oven to Gas Mark 7/220°C/425°F. Butter a 28 cm/11-inch gratin dish. Cut the dough into two pieces, one slightly larger than the other. Roll out the larger piece and line it into the dish, so that it slightly overhangs the edge. Fill this with the apple mixture. Roll out the remaining pastry and arrange it on top. Dampen the two pastry edges and roll them together to seal the pie. Make a small hole with the point of a knife in the centre of the pie to allow steam to escape during cooking.

**4** Transfer the pie to the oven and cook it for 15 minutes. Then reduce the heat to Gas Mark 4/180°C/350°F and leave it to cook for a further 20 minutes, until the top is golden brown. Serve hot or warm from the gratin dish.

# GREAT BRITAIN

Apple Pie

Buttermilk Scones

Gingerbread Cake

# QUEEN OF PUDDINGS

SERVES 6

*150 g/5 oz fresh white breadcrumbs*
*750 ml/1¼ pints milk*
*50 g/2 oz butter*
*15 mm/⅝-inch strip zest of lemon*
*3 eggs*
*150 g/5 oz caster sugar*
*3 tablespoons raspberry jam*

**1** Preheat the oven to Gas Mark 2/150°C/300°F. Sprinkle the bottom of a 28 cm/11-inch gratin dish with the breadcrumbs. Pour the milk into a medium saucepan. Add the butter and zest of lemon. Warm this up until the butter has melted.

**2** Separate the eggs. Whisk the yolks with 50 g/2 oz of the sugar, then add the warm milk. Strain this into the gratin dish. Leave to stand for 20 minutes. Then transfer the dish to the oven and leave to cook for 30 minutes until just set.

**3** Take the pudding out of the oven and leave it to cool for 10 minutes. Spread the top with the raspberry jam.

**4** Beat the egg whites to a firm snow. Beat in half the remaining sugar, then fold in the rest. Using a tablespoon, pile the meringue on top of the pudding. Transfer the pudding back into the oven and cook it for about a further 15 minutes, until the meringue is golden. Serve warm from the gratin dish.

# RED FRUIT CRUMBLE

SERVES 6

*250 g/8 oz cherries*
*200 g/7 oz redcurrants*
*125 g/4 oz strawberries*
*150 g/5 oz brown sugar*
*200 g/7 oz plain flour*
*½ teaspoon cinnamon*
*150 g/5 oz butter, unsalted*

**1** Preheat the oven to Gas Mark 6/200°C/400°F. Butter a 22 cm/8½-inch round gratin dish.

**2** Wash the fruit. Remove the stones and stalks from the cherries and pick over the redcurrants. Hull the strawberries. Put the cherries, redcurrants and strawberries into a bowl and sprinkle with 50 g/2 oz of the sugar. Mix well and turn the fruit out into the dish, arranging it in a single, tightly packed layer.

**3** Sieve the flour into a bowl. Add the remaining sugar, cinnamon and butter. Rub with your fingers and then palms for 5–6 minutes until you have a crumble mixture the consistency of large breadcrumbs. Cover the fruit with this, smoothing it out with a spatula. Transfer the dish to the oven and cook for 20–25 minutes. Serve the crumble hot or warm, with cream.

# FRUIT CAKE

In Great Britain, this traditional cake is transformed into a luxurious birthday or Christmas cake by covering it with almond paste and royal icing, then decorating it lavishly.

SERVES 6

*125 g/4 oz butter*
*125 g/4 oz brown sugar*
*1 tablespoon molasses*
*2 eggs*
*2 tablespoons cognac*
*grated zest of 1 unwaxed lemon*
*1 teaspoon vanilla essence*
*150 g/5 oz plain white flour*
*½ teaspoon baking powder*
*4 pinches of salt*
*½ teaspoon ground cinnamon*
*½ teaspoon ground ginger*
*4 pinches of grated nutmeg*
*4 pinches of ground cloves*
*50 g/2 oz candied peel*
*150 g/5 oz currants*
*150 g/5 oz sultanas*
*150 g/5 oz seedless raisins*
*50 g/2 oz glacé cherries*

For the tin:
*1 knob of butter*

**1** Grease an 18 cm/7-inch cake tin and line it with greaseproof paper which you should also grease.

**2** Place the butter in a mixing bowl and beat in the sugar and molasses until the mixture is light and creamy.

**3** Beat the eggs in a bowl, and add the cognac, the zest of the lemon and the vanilla essence. Sift the flour, baking powder, salt and spices into a second mixing bowl.

**4** Alternately add the egg mixture and the sifted flour to the mixture of butter and sugar, stirring with a spatula.

**5** Chop the candied peel and add to the cake mixture, together with the dried fruit and cherries. Mix well. Turn the cake mixture into the cake tin, levelling the top and slightly indenting the centre. Leave to rest for 1 hour.

**6** After 30 minutes, preheat the oven to Gas Mark 5/190°C/350°F. At the end of the 1 hour resting period, transfer the cake to the oven, lower the temperature to Gas Mark 2/150°C/300°F and bake for 2 hours. Allow the cake to cool in the tin before turning it out.

This cake keeps well in an airtight tin.

# TREACLE TART

SERVES 6

*375 g/12 oz shortcrust pastry*
*100 g/3 ½ oz molasses*
*100 g/3 ½ oz golden syrup*
*2 tablespoons lemon juice*
*50 g/2 oz butter*
*1 egg*
*75 g/3 oz candied peel*
*50 g/2 oz fresh white bread with crusts cut off*
*grated zest of 1 unwaxed lemon*

**1** Preheat the oven to Gas Mark 6/200°C/400°F. Grease a 24 cm/9 ½-inch flan dish with a knob of butter. Roll out the pastry and line the dish with two-thirds of the quantity. Cut the remainder of the pastry into strips 1 cm/½ inch wide.

**2** Pour the molasses, the golden syrup and the lemon juice into a saucepan and add the butter. Place over a very low heat and stir until the butter has melted. Remove from the heat.

**3** Beat the egg in a bowl. Chop the candied peel finely. Make breadcrumbs from the bread using a food processor. Add the egg to the saucepan, together with the breadcrumbs and the zest of the lemon. Mix, then pour this mixture into the pastry base. Cover in a criss-cross pattern with the strips of pastry, pressing them down at the edges of the tart so that they stick to the pastry sides.

**4** Transfer to the oven and bake for about 30 minutes until the tart is golden brown. Serve warm or cold with cream.

# GERMANY

## GERMAN CUISINE REFLECTS THE HISTORY

*of the country. But it really took off from the Middle Ages, when spices were*

introduced into the country: saffron, cinnamon, ginger, cumin, cloves, cardamom, mace and pepper. They came from the Orient, cost a great deal and their use in cookery was a sign of affluence, as was using sugar. Meat and game were flavoured with spices and so were desserts and hot wine; sugar went into savoury dishes and fruit and vegetables were used together to garnish or stuff meat: wild fruit for the most part – cranberries, redcurrants, raspberries, bilberries – which were abundant in the countryside and which the medieval Germans used to garnish the game they hunted. At the end of the seventeenth century the potato was introduced, and began to play an important role in German cuisine, soon becoming indispensable to it. Today, no German meal is complete without potato salad (*Kartoffelsalat*), or potato dumplings (*Kartoffelklösse* or *Thuringer Klösse*), or without boiled potatoes with cumin, spread with white cheese and sprinkled with dill (*Kraüter-*

*Pellkartoffeln*). Spiced cuisine and sugar used in savoury dishes are still the rule today – all over the country. Also found all over Germany are pork dishes and cooked pork meats and all varieties of cabbage. But the experience of eating in Hamburg is not the same as eating in Munich, nor in Frankfurt the same as in Berlin.

In the north, bordered by the sea, you can enjoy fish and shellfish in the Scandinavian or Polish style such as herrings in sour cream with dill pickles; meat and poultry – particularly goose – are accompanied by jellies and jams; and there is also *labskaus*, salt beef simmered, then minced and mixed with mashed potato and onions. In the middle of the country, famous for the three Ws – *Wein, Wurst und Weck* (wine, sausages and rolls) – the Westphalian ham reigns with Frankfurter sausages and roast beef marinated in raisins and spices, served with croquette potatoes, apple sauce and dried apricots: *Rheinischer Sauerbraten*.

The cuisine of southern Germany is the best known outside the country and is still really the only cuisine which represents it. Black Forest gâteau and apple strudel are cooked around the world daily. Venison marinated in red wine, with gin, orange rind and redcurrants, served with cranberry jelly, *Spätzle*, stuffed cabbage, pear, cherry and mandarin orange compôte, is a sumptuous dish and has for many years featured as one of the classic European dishes.

All of these are accompanied by good beer, the best known being that of Munich and the oldest that of Einsbeck. But each town has its own beer, from Dortmund and Düsseldorf to Berlin. And the excellent wines of the Rhine valley must not be forgotten either.

An extensive, varied, generous cuisine; rich in colours and flavours - such is the cuisine of Germany; still well known only in parts, it is worth getting to know as a whole.

# KOHLSUPPE

## *Cabbage Soup*

SERVES 6

*1 curly cabbage heart, 1.25 kg/3 lb*
*750 g/1½ lb potatoes, floury variety*
*500 g/1 lb carrots*
*2 leeks, white parts only*
*250 g/8 oz celeriac*
*250 g/8 oz lean smoked bacon*
*1 small onion*
*4 cloves*
*1 bay leaf*
*2 tablespoons chopped chives*
*salt and pepper*

**1** Rinse the cabbage heart, chop it into quarters and cut out the hard centre part. Slice each quarter into thin strips. Peel and wash the potatoes and dice them into 1 cm/½-inch cubes. Peel and wash the carrots and cut them diagonally into 5mm/¼-inch slices. Peel and rinse the leeks and cut them diagonally into 1 cm/½-inch slices. Peel and rinse the celeriac and cut it into 1 cm/½ inch cubes. Cut the bacon into small strips 1 cm/½ inch long.

**2** Put 1.5 litres/2½ pints of water into a round casserole. Stick the onion with the cloves and put it into the pot with the bay leaf. Bring to the boil, add a little salt, pepper, the bacon and all the vegetables. Bring back to the boil, cover and leave to simmer for 1 hour.

**3** When the soup is cooked, take out the onion and bay leaf. Put in the chives and give it a stir. Serve hot from the casserole.

# LINSENSUPPE

## *Lentil Soup*

In Germany they sometimes add small cubes of smoked bacon to cook with the lentils.

SERVES 4

*200 g/7 oz green lentils*
*1.25 litres/2¼ pints chicken stock*
*1 small onion*
*2 cloves*
*1 bouquet garni, consisting of 2 parsley stalks, 1 bay leaf and 1 small celery stick with leaves*
*1 garlic clove*
*1 carrot*
*salt and pepper*

**1** Rinse and drain the lentils. Put them into a medium-size round casserole and add the chicken stock.

**2** Stick the onion with the cloves. Tie up the bouquet garni. Add the onion, bouquet garni and whole garlic clove to the lentils. Peel and slice the carrot thinly and add it to the casserole. Season with pepper and slowly bring to the boil over a low heat. Leave to cook for 1 hour until the lentils are really tender. Season with salt at the end of cooking.

**3** When the lentils are ready, take out the garlic, onion and bouquet garni. The soup may be served as it is or half the quantity may be put through a blender and then mixed back in with the whole lentils; alternatively, the entire soup, including the carrot, may be put through the blender. Serve hot from a tureen with croûtons if desired.

# RINDFLEISCH MIT SCHNITTLAUCHSOSSE

## *Braised Beef in Chive Sauce*

SERVES 6

*1.5 kg/3½ lb piece of beef skirt*
*2 carrots*
*1 leek, white part only*
*1 onion*
*2 cloves*
*6 parsley stalks*
*6 pinches grated nutmeg*
*1 tablespoon white or black peppercorns*
*100 g/3½ oz thick* crème fraîche
*6 tablespoons chopped chives*
*salt and pepper*

**1** Rinse and wipe dry the meat. Put it into a large round casserole and fill with cold water to cover the meat. Bring to the boil and leave to boil up for 5 minutes. Drain and rinse the meat and pour away the cooking liquid. Rinse the pot and put the meat back in with a fresh lot of water to cover it.

**2** Peel, wash and cut the carrots into 2 cm/¾-inch slices. Wash the leek and cut it into 2 pieces. Stick the onion with the cloves. Put the carrots, leek, onion and parsley around the meat. Add half the nutmeg, the peppercorns and a little salt. Bring to the boil, then cover and leave to cook over a low heat for 3 hours, turning the meat 4 times.

**3** At the end of 3 hours, take the meat out of the pot and set it aside to keep hot. Strain the broth into a saucepan. Bring to the boil and leave to cook until it has reduced to a thick syrupy consistency: there should be about 250 ml/8 fl oz left. Add the cream, boil up for a further 2 minutes and add the chives. Stir and remove from the heat. Season with salt, pepper and the remaining nutmeg.

**4** Slice the meat thickly and arrange it on a hot serving dish. Serve immediately, handing the sauce round separately in a sauce-boat. Serve with boiled potatoes and green vegetables.

# KALBSVÖGEL

## *Stuffed Veal Rolls*

There are many variations of this recipe.

SERVES 4

*4 veal escalopes, 150 g/5 oz each: eye of fillet*
*4 teaspoons Dijon mustard*
*4 rashers lean smoked bacon, very thin cut*
*4 hard-boiled eggs*
*1 large onion*
*1 tablespoon groundnut oil*
*25 g/1 oz butter*
*125 ml/4 fl oz red wine*
*1 tablespoon tomato purée*
*250 ml/8 fl oz veal stock*
*salt and pepper*

**1** Ask the butcher to beat out the escalopes as thinly as possible. Lay 1 escalope flat and spread it with a teaspoonful of mustard. Lay 1 rasher of bacon on top and a hard-boiled egg, shelled. Wrap the egg up in the meat, pinning the edges together with wooden cocktail sticks. Repeat for the remaining escalopes. Season all 4 with salt and pepper.

**2** Finely chop the onion. Heat the oil in a shallow casserole, such as a cassadou. Put in the butter and when it has melted, brown the veal rolls on all sides. Take them out, set them aside on a plate and put in the onion. Stirring continuously, fry the onion until it just turns golden. Put the veal rolls back in and sprinkle in the wine. When the wine has evaporated, add the tomato purée. Mix well, and then pour on the veal stock. Bring to the boil, cover and leave to cook on a low heat for 1 hour, turning the veal rolls several times during cooking.

**3** When the veal rolls are cooked, take them out with a slotted spoon and arrange them on a serving dish to keep hot. Boil up the cooking liquid to reduce it until syrupy and coat the veal rolls with this sauce. Serve immediately.

# KÖNIGSBERGER KLOPSE

## *Meatballs in Caper Sauce*

SERVES 6

For the meatballs:
*50 g/2 oz stale white bread*
*100 ml/3½ fl oz chicken or meat stock*
*300 g/10 oz minced pork*
*200 g/7 oz minced beef*
*1 small onion*
*zest of 1 unwaxed lemon*
*1 egg*
*salt and pepper*

To cook:
*750 ml/1¼ pints chicken or meat stock*
*2 egg yolks*
*2 tablespoons lemon juice*
*½ teaspoon made English mustard*
*1 tablespoon thick* crème fraîche
*2 tablespoons capers, drained*
*2 tablespoons chopped flat-leaf parsley*
*salt and pepper*

**1** Make the meatballs: crumble the bread into a bowl and add the stock. Leave to absorb the liquid and swell for 10 minutes. Mix the two kinds of mince together in a bowl. Finely chop the onion. Add it to the meat mixture together with the zest of lemon, salt and pepper. Put in the breadcrumbs and egg and stir well. Form the mixture into meatballs about 4 cm/1½ inches round, rolling them between dampened hands.

**2** Bring the stock to the boil in a large saucepan. Drop in the meatballs and leave them to cook for 30 minutes, turning them with a draining spoon. Remove them with the draining spoon and set them aside to keep hot.

**3** Boil the cooking liquid to reduce it to 500 ml/ 18 fl oz. Strain it into a clean, smaller saucepan. Beat the egg yolks with the lemon juice, mustard and cream. Pour this into the hot stock and, stirring continuously, cook on a low heat until thickened, without allowing it to boil. When the sauce has reached a smooth consistency, remove the pan from the heat and add the capers and parsley. Add salt and pepper if necessary. Coat the meatballs with the sauce and serve.

# FISCH IM OFEN GEBACKEN MIT WEISSWEIN

## *Baked Fish in White Wine*

SERVES 4

*1 flat fish, 1.25 kg/3 lb: brill, sole, young turbot or plaice*
*4 shallots*
*50 g/2 oz butter*
*300 ml/½ pint dry white wine*
*100 g/3½ oz thick* crème fraîche
*salt and pepper*

**1** Ask the fishmonger to gut and skin the fish. Rinse it and wipe dry. Season with salt and pepper. Finely chop the shallots.

**2** Preheat the oven to Gas Mark 7/220°C/425°F. Using half the butter, grease a gratin dish just large enough to hold the fish. Spread half the shallots on the bottom, lay the fish on top and cover with the remaining shallots.

**3** Mix the wine and cream together, season and pour on to the fish. Dot with the remaining butter and transfer the dish to the oven. Leave to cook for 25–30 minutes: at the end of the cooking time if a small knife blade inserted between the fillets lifts them easily from the bone, the fish is done. Serve hot from the gratin dish.

# Germany

Königsberger Klopse
*(Meatballs in Caper Sauce)*

Hasenpfeffer
*(Jugged Hare)*

Kalbsvögel
*(Stuffed Veal Rolls)*

Kartoffelklosse
*(Potato Dumplings)*

# HASENPFEFFER

## *Jugged Hare*

SERVES 6

*1 hare, 2 kg/4½ lb*
*1 onion*
*1 carrot*
*750 ml/1¼ pints red wine*
*100 ml/3½ fl oz wine vinegar*
*3 tablespoons cognac*
*1 sprig thyme*
*1 bay leaf*
*1 tablespoon crushed peppercorns*
*200 g/7 oz lean smoked bacon*
*3 tablespoons oil*
*18 pickling onions*
*1 tablespoon flour*
*3 tablespoons redcurrant jelly*
*salt and pepper*

**1** Ask the butcher to cut the hare into 9 pieces. Rinse it and wipe dry. Season with salt and pepper. Finely chop the onion. Peel, wash and slice the carrot thinly.

**2** Pour the wine, vinegar and cognac into a large bowl. Add the onion, carrot, thyme and bay leaf, crumbling the last two in your fingers. Add the crushed peppercorns. Put the hare pieces into this marinade and leave them to marinate for 12 hours in the refrigerator, turning them several times during this period.

**3** At the end of 12 hours take the bowl out of the refrigerator and drain the meat. Wipe it dry. Strain the marinade and remove the spices. Reserve the marinade.

**4** Cut the bacon into thin slivers.

**5** Heat the oil in a large oval casserole and lightly brown the pieces of hare on all sides for 10 minutes. Add the bacon and pickling onions and stir for another 5 minutes until the meat is well browned. Dust with flour and cook for a further minute, still stirring.

**6** Pour the marinade into the casserole, bring to the boil, cover and cook for 2 hours on a very low heat, stirring from time to time.

**7** When the hare is cooked, take the pieces out with a draining spoon and set them aside to keep hot in a deep dish. Stir the redcurrant jelly into the cooking juices until it has melted. Coat the pieces of hare with this sauce and serve immediately.

# KARTOFFELKLÖSSE

## *Potato Dumplings*

These dumplings may be made a number of ways: simply with cooked or raw potato; with the addition of tiny cubes of bread or fried bacon cubes. This is the classic version.

SERVES 6

*1.5 kg/3½ lb potatoes, floury variety*
*2 eggs*
*150 g/5 oz plain flour*
*75 g/3 oz butter, melted*
*salt and pepper*

**1** Peel and rinse the potatoes. Finely grate half of them. Wrap the grated potatoes in a cloth, knot it and hang it up to drain the liquid out of them.

**2** Cook the remaining potatoes in salted water for about 20 minutes until very tender. Put them though a sieve, blender or food processor and transfer then to a bowl. Add the grated raw potatoes. Stir in the eggs and flour and mix well until you have a smooth mixture.

**3** Using two soup spoons, form the mixture into dumplings. Boil some salted water in a large saucepan. Drop the dumplings in and leave them to cook for 20 minutes, turning them over with a draining spoon. When cooked, remove them with a draining spoon, sprinkle them with melted butter and serve hot. Season with pepper at the table.

# APFELROTKOHL

## *Red Cabbage with Apple*

SERVES 4-6

*1 red cabbage, 1.5 kg/3½ lb*
*150 ml/¼ pint red wine vinegar*
*2 tablespoons caster sugar*
*1 teaspoon salt*
*2 cooking apples*
*1 onion*
*25 g/1 oz lard*
*1 bay leaf*
*6 juniper berries*
*2 cloves*
*3 tablespoons red wine*
*3 tablespoons redcurrant jelly*
*salt and pepper*

1 Cut the cabbage into quarters, wash it and remove the hard centre. Thinly slice each quarter, widthways. Put it into a bowl and add the vinegar to preserve the red colour and the sugar and salt. Mix well.

2 Cut the apples into quarters and core them; cut each quarter into 3 mm/⅛-inch strips. Finely chop the onion.

3 Melt the lard in a large round casserole. Put in the apple and onion and, stirring continuously, cook until golden coloured. Add the cabbage and mix well. Add 250 ml/8 fl oz of boiling water and the bay leaf, juniper berries, cloves, salt and pepper. Lower the heat, cover the casserole and leave to cook on a very low heat for 2 hours, stirring from time to time. If it dries out too quickly, add a few tablespoons of water as necessary during cooking.

4 When the cabbage is cooked, there should be no liquid left in the pot. Take out the bay leaf. Add the wine and redcurrant jelly, stir until the jelly has melted and serve immediately.

# GEWÜRZKUCHEN

## *Spicy Cake*

SERVES 6

*150 g/5 oz unsalted butter*
*200 g/7 oz caster sugar*
*4 eggs*
*1 teaspoon vanilla essence*
*150 g/5 oz plain flour*
*1 teaspoon grated nutmeg*
*1 teaspoon ground cinnamon*
*1 teaspoon ground cloves*
*40 g/1½ oz unsweetened cocoa powder*
*2 teaspoons baking powder*
*150 g/5 oz ground almonds*
*250 ml/8 fl oz milk*
*icing sugar, to serve*

1 Preheat the oven to Gas Mark 4/180°C/350°F. Butter an oblong cake tin 28 x 11 cm/11 x 4 inches in size.

2 Put the butter into a bowl and add the sugar in a stream. Beat with a fork until the mixture whitens. Separate the eggs. Add the yolks, one by one, to the butter and sugar mixture. Add the vanilla essence.

3 Sieve the flour, spices, cocoa and baking powder in a bowl. Add this to the previous mixture, folding it in with a spatula. Then add the ground almonds, followed by the milk, and stir well.

4 Beat the egg whites to a firm snow and fold them into the mixture with a spatula.

5 Turn the mixture out into the cake tin and put it in the oven. Leave to cook for 1¼ hours until the cake has risen and the point of a knife inserted in the centre comes out clean. Leave the cake to stand for 10 minutes in the tin before turning it out. Leave to go cold on a wire rack before serving dusted with icing sugar.

# SCHWARZWÄLDER KIRSCHTORTE

## *Black Forest Gâteau*

SERVES 8

For the sponge cakes:
*6 eggs*
*200 g/7 oz caster sugar*
*1 teaspoon vanilla essence*
*65 g/2½ oz plain flour*
*75 g/3 oz unsweetened cocoa powder*
*125 g/4 oz melted butter, cooled*

For the sugar syrup:
*100 g/3½ oz caster sugar*
*100 ml/3½ fl oz water*
*100 ml/3½ fl oz kirsch*

For the filling:
*750 ml/1¼ pints whipping cream, chilled*
*2 tablespoons caster sugar*
*1 tablespoon vanilla sugar*
*500 g/1 lb morello cherries, pitted, or 2 x 425 g*
*(14 oz) can of pitted morello cherries*

To decorate:
*maraschino cherries*
*chocolate shavings*

1  Make the sponge cakes: preheat the oven to Gas Mark 6/200°C/400°F. Break the eggs into a bowl and add the sugar in a stream. Beat with an electric whisk for 5 minutes until the mixture is fluffy and whitened. Add the vanilla. Sieve the flour and cocoa into the bowl, whisking them in gently. Finally beat in the melted butter.

2  Butter 3 cake tins 22 cm/8½ inches in diameter and divide the mixture between them. Transfer them to the hot oven and cook for 15–18 minutes until the mixture has risen but is springy when touched. Take them out of the oven and leave to stand for 2 minutes before turning them out and cooling them on wire racks. If you only have one cake tin, bake one after the other.

3  Make the sugar syrup: put the sugar, water and 4 tablespoons of the juice from the cherries used for the filling into a saucepan. Bring slowly to the boil

on a low heat and continue to simmer for 5 minutes. Remove from the heat and leave to cool before adding the kirsch.

4  Prick the sponge cakes a few times with a needle and moisten them with the syrup on both sides. Leave to go cold.

5  Prepare the filling: whip the cream until it forms little peaks between the tines of a fork. Add the sugar and vanilla sugar, beating continuously until you have a firm chantilly cream.

6  Assemble the cake: arrange 1 sponge base on a cake dish and spread it with a little of the chantilly cream. Sprinkle with half the cherries and cover with more chantilly cream. Arrange the second sponge on this and garnish in the same way. Put the last sponge on top and cover the whole of the gâteau in chantilly cream using either a spatula or a forcing bag with a large nozzle. Place it in the refrigerator and leave for 6 hours before serving.

7  When ready to serve, decorate the Black Forest gâteau with cherries and chocolate shavings.

# IRELAND

*ERIN THE GREEN, THE COUNTRY OF LIGHT*
*filtering through soft curtains of rain, with its 3,000 km of coastline and nearly*

140,000 hectares of rivers, lakes and streams is a country where water is part of the landscape and fishing is an important part of life. Fish and shellfish – herrings, cod, trout, mackerel, dabs, sole, lobster, crayfish and crabs – abound around the coast. The salmon is exquisite, the oysters wonderful and the mussels plump and tasty. But the majority of this harvest of the sea is exported. The Irish themselves prefer the tender, tasty meat of the lamb and beef grazing on their green pastures. It is served grilled or stewed, sometimes marinated in beer and spices, and served with the king of vegetables, the potato - the staple food of Irish cookery.

The Irish are the biggest consumers of potatoes in Europe. In their lush fields grow the best potatoes in the world. Watered by the spray off the sea they have a flavour which is delicious. Irish cabbages, turnips, onions, sugar beet and cereals are good too: wheat for making bread, corn for the horses, and barley for the famous Irish beers– lagers, ales, porters and stouts – such as Guinness (the best known abroad) and the no less famous whisky. All these drinks have had a great influence on the simple, tasty cookery of Ireland which is based on the country's own delicious produce. This tiny land of savoury dishes gave birth to Irish stew – made with mutton, and to hot-pot – made with beef, veal, rabbit or chicken, to other delicious stews with potatoes and onions and to beef with brown ale: all recipes which can be successfully made anywhere in Europe. As for Irish coffee, it flows throughout the world.

## COCKLE SOUP

SERVES 4

*1.5 kg/3½ lb cockles*
*100 g/3½ oz onions*
*1 celery heart*
*50 g/2 oz butter*
*2 tablespoons chopped flat-leaf parsley*
*500 ml/18 fl oz milk*
*1 teaspoon arrowroot*
*1 egg yolk*
*100 ml/3½ fl oz single cream*
*pepper*

**1** Rinse the cockles and leave them to soak for 1 hour in cold water to remove any sand they may contain.

**2** Finely chop the onions. Cut the celery into thin slices. Reserve 1 tablespoon of the leaves for a garnish.

**3** Melt the butter in a large round casserole. Put in the onions and lightly brown them on a low heat. Add the celery and parsley and stir for 1 minute. Drain the cockles and drop them into the pot. Pour in 250 ml/8 fl oz of water and stir. As soon as the cockles have opened, remove them with a draining spoon and set them aside in a bowl. Discard any that do not open.

**4** Add the milk to the cooking liquid and leave to cook for 10 minutes. Dilute the arrowroot in 2 tablespoons of cold water and stir it into the pot. Leave to boil up for 3 minutes until the mixture thickens. Remove the cockle shells and put the cockles in; heat the soup through on a low heat.

**5** Beat the egg yolk and cream together. Pour this into the soup and stir until a smooth consistency is obtained, without allowing the mixture to boil. Turn it into a soup tureen, garnish with the celery leaves and serve hot. Add pepper at the table.

## GRILLED SALMON WITH MUSTARD SAUCE

SERVES 6

*6 thick slices salmon fillet with skin*
*3 shallots*
*2 tablespoons pure, clear alcohol vinegar*
*1 tablespoon English mustard powder*
*1 tablespoon mustard seeds*
*200 ml/7 fl oz chicken consommé*
*2 egg yolks*
*125 ml/4 fl oz double cream*
*2 tablespoons port*
*1 tablespoon chopped fresh fennel*
*salt and pepper*

**1** Rinse and wipe dry the salmon. Season it with salt and pepper.

**2** Cook the salmon by dry frying it in a marmitout frying pan, skin side down. Cook it for 20 minutes on a low heat.

**3** Finely chop the shallots. Put them into the marmitout saucepan with the vinegar. Put the pan on a low heat and leave the vinegar to evaporate. Vigorously whisk in the mustard powder, mustard seeds and consommé. Bring to the boil.

**4** Whisk the egg yolks in a bowl with the cream and port. Pour this into the marmitout saucepan, whisking continuously. Remove from the heat. Add the fennel, stir and keep warm.

**5** Divide the salmon between 4 hot plates and serve with the sauce in a sauce-boat and with boiled potatoes or boxty (page 132).

# BEEF IN GUINNESS WITH PRUNES

SERVES 6

*12 prunes*
*1.5 kg/3½ lb braising beef*
*1 onion*
*250 g/8 oz carrots*
*2 tablespoons groundnut oil*
*1 tablespoon chopped flat-leaf parsley*
*2 tablespoons flour*
*250 ml/8 fl oz Guinness*
*2 tablespoons chopped hazelnuts*
*salt and pepper*

**1** Soak the prunes until they are needed in enough hot water to cover them. Cut the meat into 4 cm/1½-inch cubes. Chop the onion. Peel, rinse and wipe dry the carrots and cut them into thick slices.

**2** Heat the oil in a large round cocotte. Put in the meat and brown it on all sides. Add the onion, carrots and parsley and stir for 1 minute. Dust with flour and stir until the flour is browned.

**3** Pour the Guinness into the pot and add enough water to just cover the meat. Add salt and pepper. Bring to the boil, turn down the heat and leave to simmer for 2½ hours.

**4** Meanwhile, brown the hazelnuts in a dry pan. Drain the prunes, open them up without splitting them in half and stone them. Fill each prune with hazelnuts.

**5** At the end of the meat cooking time, give the contents of the pot a stir and add the stuffed prunes. Simmer for a further 30 minutes before serving hot from the oven dish.

# SPICED BEEF

Traditionally served at Christmas time.

SERVES 6

*2 bay leaves*
*4 cloves*
*2 mace blades*
*2 tablespoons crushed peppercorns*
*2 garlic cloves*
*1 tablespoon sugar*
*4 tablespoons rock salt*
*1.5 kg/3½ lb beef (brisket)*

To cook:
*1 onion*
*250 g/8 oz carrots*
*1 bouquet garni, consisting of 1 bay leaf, 1 sprig thyme and 6 parsley stalks*
*250 ml/8 fl oz Guinness*

**1** Put the bay leaves, cloves, mace, pepper and garlic cloves (crushed flat with the back of a fork), sugar and salt into a large bowl. Mix well and put in the meat. Turn the meat in this marinade and leave it to marinate for 24 hours in the refrigerator, turning several times.

**2** At the end of 24 hours, rinse the meat and wipe it dry. Put it into a large round casserole. Chop the onion. Peel, rinse and chop the carrots into 5 mm/¼-inch slices. Arrange these vegetables around the meat and put in the bouquet garni. Add the Guinness and enough water to just cover the meat. Bring to the boil on a low heat and leave to simmer for 5 hours. Turn the meat once during cooking.

**3** At the end of this time take out the meat and leave it to go cold. Serve cold, thinly sliced, with pickles.

# EIRE

Cockle Soup

Boxty

Grilled Salmon in
Mustard Sauce

# COLCANNON

SERVES 6

*500 g/1 lb potatoes, floury variety*
*500 g/1 lb savoy cabbage*
*2 leeks, white parts only, or 6 spring onions*
*100 g/3½ oz butter*
*250 ml/8 fl oz milk*
*salt and pepper*

**1** Wash the potatoes and put them into a saucepan. Cover with cold water and bring to the boil. Season with salt and leave to cook for about 20 minutes until they are really tender.

**2** Slice the cabbage into 5 mm/¼-inch strips and cook it in boiling salted water for 5 minutes. Drain.

**3** Rinse the leeks or spring onions and slice them finely. Melt half the butter in a large cocotte and cook the leeks or onions until they are lightly browned, stirring continuously. Add the milk and cabbage and mix well.

**4** Drain and peel the potatoes and put them through a blender or food processor. Add them to the pot, stir and season with salt and pepper. Stir in the remaining butter and serve hot.

# BOXTY

SERVES 6

*1 kg/2 lb potatoes, floury variety*
*100 g/3½ oz flour*
*100 to 150 ml/3½–5 fl oz milk*
*75 g/3 oz butter*
*salt*

**1** Peel and rinse the potatoes. Boil half of them in salted water for about 20 minutes until they are really tender. Put them through a blender or food processor and then into a bowl.

**2** Grate the remaining potato finely. Add this to the cooked potato in the bowl. Mix well, incorporating the flour and milk until you have a smooth mixture.

**3** Melt the butter in a large non-stick frying pan. Cook the potato cakes, in spoonfuls, for 4 minutes each side until they are golden brown. Serve hot.

# BARM BRACK

This fruit bread is traditionally made for All Saints' Eve, 31st October. A gold ring is hidden in the dough and whoever finds it will supposedly get married within the year.

SERVES 6

*½ packet dried yeast, 15 g/½ oz*
*100 ml/3½ fl oz warm milk*
*50 g/2 oz caster sugar*
*250 g/8 oz plain flour*
*½ teaspoon cinnamon*
*¼ teaspoon nutmeg*
*½ teaspoon salt*
*1 small egg*
*50 g/2 oz unsalted butter, melted*
*65 g/2½ oz mixed raisins and sultanas*
*40 g/1½ oz candied peel*

For the icing:
*2 tablespoons caster sugar*
*1 tablespoon boiling water*

**1** Soften the yeast in 2 tablespoons of the milk with 1 teaspoon of the sugar. Leave to rise for 10 minutes.

**2** Sieve the flour, spices and salt into a bowl. Add the remaining sugar, remaining milk and the yeast. Beat the egg and add it to the bowl with the cooled melted butter. Mix well, working the dough for 5 minutes until it is elastic and pulls away from the sides of the bowl. Cover with a damp tea towel and leave to rise in a warm place for 1 hour.

**3** When the dough has risen, add the raisins and chopped candied peel, working them in very fast. Butter a 500 g/1 lb loaf tin and put in the dough. Leave to rise again in a warm place for 30 minutes.

**4** Preheat the oven to Gas Mark 6/200°C/400°F. When the dough has risen transfer the tin to the oven and bake for 25 minutes. Reduce the heat to Gas Mark 5/190°C/375°F and bake for a further 15 minutes.

**5** At the end of this time, make the icing: melt the sugar in 1 tablespoon of boiling water and brush this over the top and visible sides of the bread. Put it back into the oven and bake for a further 5 minutes.

**6** When the barm brack is cooked, take it out of the oven and leave to stand for 10 minutes before turning it out of the tin. Leave to cool on a wire rack. Serve sliced, plain or with butter. The barm brack may also be lightly toasted and buttered.

# LUXEMBOURG

*A STRIP OF LAND SURROUNDED BY*

*much larger countries, some of which have occupied it and others divided it,*

Luxembourg lived, up until the nineteenth century, off its forests and a land which was not rich enough to grow cereals. Here was plain country cooking, the foundations of which were 'marsh beans' – those huge dried beans which are the main ingredient of the famous *tirtech* (smoked collar of pork with beans) – and peas and potatoes, which were introduced into the country in the seventeenth century and very soon became a staple vegetable. Today potatoes are served with all meat dishes, either mashed with chives or cabbage or in the form of *cebeulte kartoffeln*, cubes of cooked potatoes in a casserole with fried strips of bacon. They grew a little wheat, corn, rye, barley, German wheat and buckwheat, the main ingredient of *sterzelen* – dark patties which replaced bread when corn was short – and those sugary pancakes generally made today with wheat flour.

With the arrival of better days, the cuisine of Luxembourg was laid open to external influences and gourmand tastes became permissible. If fruit and vegetables are not always satisfying, everything needed to make grander gourmet dishes can be found here – including beer and the lovely Luxembourg Moselle wines which cooks use a great deal and which are named after their types of vine. Elbing, dry and light, which is served with smoked pork and beans and used in white stews and chicken and rice dishes; Riesling, the basis of fish stock for pike, prawns and blue trout and used in sauces for sweetbreads and *moules marinières*; the round and fruity Rivaner or the smooth Auxerrois, sometimes used instead of Riesling. And while Pinot blanc goes well with fish and shellfish and Pinot gris is delicious with roast meats and cheeses, Gewürztraminer remains the best dessert wine and is served with the famous pear, apple or plum tarts.

Nowhere in Europe is more scrupulous and loving care taken to match food and wine, an essential part of serving a good meal – a lesson which may be learnt from a country which created its own cuisine by appreciating that of others.

# BOUNESCHLUPP

## *Vegetable Soup*

'Bouneschlupp' is a term used for all soups containing green beans; they may have a few drops of wine vinegar added.

SERVES 6

*2 leeks*
*2 carrots*
*500 g/1 lb potatoes, firm variety*
*250 g/8 oz celeriac*
*500 g/1 lb green beans*
*150 g/5 oz potatoes, floury variety*
*25 g/1 oz butter*
*1 litre/1 ¾ pints chicken stock*
*4 sprigs fresh savory*
*125 ml/4 fl oz thick crème fraîche*
*salt and pepper*

**1** Peel, wash and cut the leeks into thin slices. Peel the carrots, firm potatoes and celeriac. Wash the vegetables and dice them. Wash, string and halve the green beans. Peel the floury potatoes, wash and grate them using the fine side of the grater.

**2** Melt the butter in a large round cocotte or saucepan and put in the leeks, carrots and celeriac. Stir for 5 minutes until the vegetables just start to turn golden and then add the stock. Bring to the boil, add the savory, both kinds of potato and the green beans. Salt lightly and cover the cocotte. Leave the soup to cook for 45 minutes until the vegetables are soft and the grated potato has thickened it.

**3** When the soup is cooked, remove the cocotte from the heat and add the cream. Stir well. Pour it into a soup tureen and serve. Pepper may be added on serving.

# KNIDDELEN

## *Buckwheat Quenelles*

SERVES 6

*200 g/7 oz white flour*
*50 g/2 oz buckwheat flour*
*2 pinches salt*
*2 eggs*
*3 tablespoons milk*
*100 g/3½ oz lean smoked bacon*
*75 g/3 oz butter*

**1** Sieve the flours into a bowl. Add the salt and make a well in the centre. Put in the eggs and milk and mix well. Work the dough by hand until it is supple and does not stick to the fingers. Wrap it in clingfilm and leave to stand for 1 hour.

**2** Meanwhile, chop the bacon, removing the rind. Melt the butter in a large frying pan and put in the bacon. Cook on a low heat until it is just turning brown.

**3** When the dough has stood for 1 hour, boil some salted water in a large saucepan. Make small barrel shapes 4 x 2 cm/1½ x ¾ inches in size out of the dough, using 2 teaspoons, and drop them into the boiling water. Leave them to cook until they rise to the surface, about 7–8 minutes. As soon as they are cooked, plunge them into really cold water, then drain them again and set them aside on a hot dish.

**4** Reheat the bacon and butter and pop the quenelles into the bacon pan. Stir gently for 2 minutes on a low heat to heat the quenelles through. Serve immediately.

# JUDD MAT GAARDEBOUNEN

## *Smoked Pork with Broad Beans*

This recipe is the national dish of Luxembourg.

SERVES 6

*1.5 kg/3½ lb smoked chine of pork*
*1 carrot*
*1 onion*
*2 celery sticks*
*2 layers of leek*
*2 cloves*

For the broad beans:
*2.5 kg/5½ lb fresh broad beans*
*100 g/3½ oz lean smoked bacon*
*100 g/3½ oz onions*
*25 g/1 oz butter*
*1 sprig fresh savory*
*200 ml/7 fl oz water*
*salt and pepper*

**1** Prepare the meat: place it in a large round casserole and cover it with cold water. Peel the carrot and wash it, together with the onion, celery and leek. Stick the onion with the cloves. Arrange these vegetables around the meat and bring to the boil. Leave to simmer for 2½ hours, removing any scum from the surface during the first 10 minutes of cooking.

**2** One hour before the end of the cooking time, prepare the beans: shell them, removing the little bitter tops. Roughly chop the smoked bacon and chop the onions.

**3** Melt the butter in a large saucepan. Put in the onion and bacon, and cook until uniformly and lightly browned, stirring continuously with a wooden spatula. Add the beans and the savory leaves and season lightly with salt and pepper. Stir for 2 minutes, then add the water. Cover the casserole and leave to simmer for 30 minutes, or until the beans are tender.

**4** When the meat is cooked, drain and slice it. Put it on a serving dish. Turn the beans into a deep serving dish and serve immediately.

# KROKETTEN

## *Croquette Potatoes*

These croquette potatoes go well with all kinds of poultry and roast meat.

SERVES 6

*500 g/1 lb potatoes, floury variety*
*100 g/3½ oz butter*
*2 eggs*
*3 tablespoons flour*
*2 tablespoons groundnut oil*
*salt*

**1** Wash the potatoes and place them in a saucepan. Cover them with cold water and bring to the boil. Leave to cook for about 20 minutes, until they are really tender. Salt during cooking.

**2** Drain the potatoes, peel them and put them through a food processor or blender for just a few seconds until smooth. Mix in half the butter and 1 egg. Stir well and leave to go cold.

**3** Put the flour into a deep dish. Beat the remaining egg in a separate dish. Using 2 tablespoons, make 12 croquette shapes out of the potato, dipping them into the flour and then into the egg.

**4** Heat the oil in a 25 cm/10-inch non-stick frying pan. Put in the remaining butter and when it has melted, cook the croquettes for about 6 minutes, turning them with a wooden spatula until browned on all sides.

**5** Remove the croquettes from the pan with the spatula, drain them quickly on kitchen paper and serve really hot.

# BUREGRESS ZALOT

## *Watercress salad*

SERVES 4

*1 floury potato weighing 100 g/3 ½ oz*
*200 g/7 oz watercress*
*½ teaspoon Dijon mustard*
*2 tablespoons white wine vinegar*
*4 tablespoons groundnut oil*
*salt and pepper*

**1** Wash the potato and place it in a saucepan. Cover with cold water and bring to the boil. Add salt and leave to cook for about 20 minutes until the tip of a knife can easily be inserted into the potato. Drain and allow to cool.

**2** Wash the cress and shake it dry, then place it in a salad bowl.

**3** Place the mustard in a bowl and add the vinegar, whipping it with a fork. Incorporate the oil while continuing to whip. Mash the potato finely with a fork and add it to the vinaigrette. Mix rapidly and tip this sauce over the salad. Mix well and serve immediately.

# QUETSCHEFLUED

## *Red Plum Tart*

SERVES 6

*3 tablespoons warm water*
*65 g/2½ oz caster sugar*
*1 teaspoon dried baker's yeast*
*125 g/4 oz plain flour*
*1 pinch salt*
*3 tablespoons milk*
*50 g/2 oz butter*
*750 g/1½ lb red plums*

**1** Put the water and 1 tablespoon of the sugar into a 200 ml/7 fl oz glass. Stir until the sugar has dissolved, then add the yeast. Stir again and leave to stand for about 10 minutes until the yeast has doubled in volume.

**2** Sieve the flour and salt into a bowl, make a well in the centre and put in the milk and yeast. Work the dough with a spatula, then knead it by hand until it is supple and no longer clings to the fingers. Melt 25 g/1 oz of the butter and add it towards the end of the kneading time. Cover the bowl and leave the dough to stand in a warm place for 1 hour.

**3** When the dough has risen, set the oven to Gas Mark 6/200°C/400°F. Butter a 25 cm/10-inch tart tin. Press the dough out with your hands and use it to line the tin. Leave the tart to stand for 10 minutes before dusting it with half the remaining sugar.

**4** Rinse, halve and stone the plums. Arrange them on top of the pastry, skin side down. Dot with the remaining butter and dust with the last of the sugar. Transfer the tart to the oven and leave it to cook for 30 minutes.

**5** When it is cooked, transfer the plum tart to a serving dish and serve it warm.

# LUXEMBOURG

Quetscheflued
*(Red Plum Tart)*

# LE CREUSET RANGE

## FRYING PANS, OMELETTE PANS AND SKILLETS

**Non-Stick Frying Pan**

| | Wooden handle | |
|---|---|---|
| 2016.23 | 9"/23cm |
| 2016.26 | 10 ¼"/26cm |
| 2016.29 | 11 ⅛"/29cm |
| 3016.26 | Lid for 26cm Frypan |

**Non-Stick Omelette Pan**

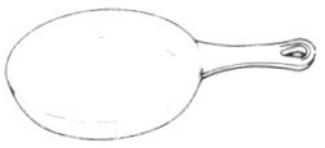

| | Iron handle | |
|---|---|---|
| 2036.20 | 8"/20cm |
| 2036.24 | 9 ½"/24cm |

**Non-Stick Skillet**

| | Iron handle | |
|---|---|---|
| 2051.23 | 9"/23cm |
| 2051.26 | 10 ¼"/26cm |

## SAUCEPANS

**Non-Stick Milk Pan**

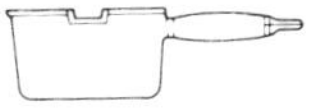

| | Wooden handle | |
|---|---|---|
| 2005.16 | 2pt/1.1L |

**Saucepan**

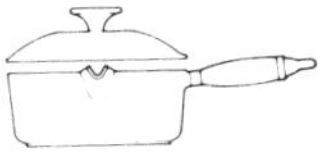

| | Wooden handle | |
|---|---|---|
| 2539.14 | 1 ¼pt/0.7L |
| 2539.16 | 2pt/1.1L |
| 2539.18 | 2 ⅔pt/1.5L |
| 2539.20 | 3 ⅓pt/1.9L |
| 2539.22 | 4 ¾pt/2.7L |

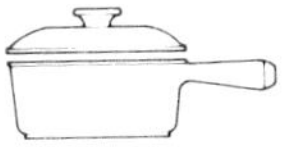

| | Iron handle | |
|---|---|---|
| 2507.16 | 2pt/1.1L |
| 2507.18 | 2 ⅔pt/1.5L |
| 2507.20 | 3 ⅓pt/1.9L |
| 2507.22 | 4 ¾pt/2.7L |

## MARMITOUTS

**Marmitout Pan**
- *Non stick lid/frying pan, Enamelled base.*

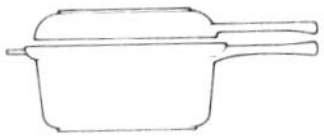

| 1531.18 | 1 ¾pt/1.0L |
|---|---|
| 1531.22 | 3pt/1.8L |
| 1531.26 | 5 ¼pt/3.0L |

**Marmitout Casserole**

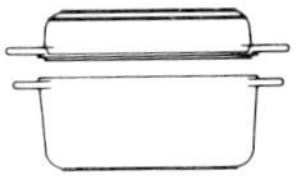

| 2581.24 | Round | |
|---|---|---|
| Lid | 3pt/1.7L |
| Base | 7pt/4.1L |

**Marmitout Roaster**

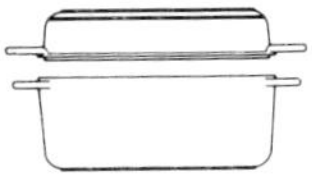

| 2582.27 | Oval | |
|---|---|---|
| Lid | 3 ¼/1.8L |
| Base | 7 ¼pt/4.2L |

## COCOTTES AND CASSEROLES

**Round Cocotte**

| 2501.18 | 3 ⅓pt/1.9L |
|---|---|
| 2501.20 | 4 ½pt/2.6L |
| 2501.22 | 6pt/3.4L |
| 2501.24 | 7 ½pt/4.3L |
| 2501.26 | 9 ½pt/5.5L |
| 2501.28 | 12pt/6.8L |
| 2501.30 | 14 ¾pt/8.4L |
| 2501.34 | 21 ½pt/12.3L |

**Oval Cocotte**

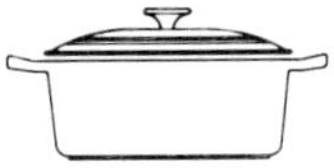

| 2502.25 | 5 ¾pt/3.3L |
|---|---|
| 2502.27 | 7 ¼pt/4.2L |
| 2502.29 | 8 ¼pt/4.8L |
| 2502.30 | 9 ¼pt/5.3L |
| 2502.31 | 11 ¼pt/6.5L |
| 2502.35 | 15 ¾pt/9.0L |

**Round Casserole**

| 2515.14 | ¾pt/0.5L |
|---|---|
| 2515.18 | 1 ¾pt/1.0L |
| 2515.22 | 3pt/1.8L |

**Casserole D'Amour**

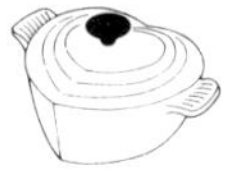

| 2510 | 4 ½pt/2.6L |
|---|---|

**Oval Casserole**

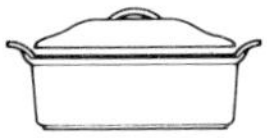

| 2506.22 | 3pt/1.8L |
|---|---|
| 2506.26 | 4 ⅓pt/2.5L |

**Buffet Casserole**

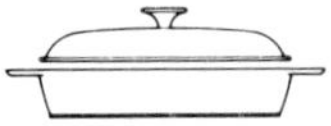

| 2532.26 | 3 ½pt/2.0L |
|---|---|
| 2532.30 | 6pt/3.4L |

## GRATINS AND OVEN DISHES

**Oval Gratin**

| 0013.20 | 8"/20cm |
|---|---|
| 0013.24 | 9 ½"/24cm |
| 0013.28 | 11"/28cm |
| 0013.32 | 12 ½"/32cm |
| 0013.36 | 14"/36cm |

**Round Gratin**

| 2010.15 | 6"/15cm |
|---|---|
| 2010.18 | 7"/18cm |
| 2010.22 | 8 ⅔"/22cm |

**Rectangular Oven Dish**

| 2011.30 | 11 ¾" x 8"/ 30 x 20cm |
|---|---|
| 2011.40 | 15 ¾" x 10"/ 40 x 25cm |

**Egg Plate**

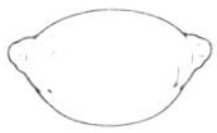

| 2009.03 | 6 ¼"/16cm |
|---|---|

**Pâté Terrine**

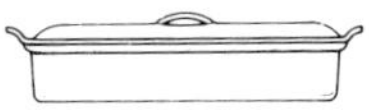

| 2524.28 | 2pt/1.1L |
|---|---|
| 2524.32 | 2 ½pt/1.4L |

## LE CREUSET SETS

**2439** • 5 Wooden handled Saucepans 14, 16, 18, 20 & 22cm plus Pine Rack
**2433** • 3 Wooden handled Saucepans 16, 18 & 20cm plus Pine Rack.
**2541** • 3 Wooden handled Saucepans 16, 18 & 20cm Non-stick Frying Pan, 4 ½pt/2.6L Round Casserole plus Pine Rack.

## FONDUE SETS

**6000** • Iron handled, Dual-function, 6 forks, Firestar burner 1 ¼pt/0.7L
**6010** • Dual function, Compact storage facility, Firestar burner 1 ¼ pt/0.7L
**6030** • Phenolic handled, Dual-function, 6 forks, Firestar burner 1 ¼pt/0.7L
**3610** • Cheese, 6 forks, alcohol heater 3 ½pt/2.0L
**6800** • Chocolate, 4 forks candle heater ½pt/0.28L
**6080** • Dual function, Oval Cast Iron pot, Cast Iron stand, 6 forks, Firestar burner 1 ¼pt/0.7L
**3620** • Dual function, Hexagonal Cast Iron pot, Cast Iron stand, 6 forks, Firestar burner 1 ¼pt/0.7L
**63809** • Wooden fondue turntable with 6 earthenware crudité/dips dishes.
**6575** • Pack of 6 Fondue forks
**6590** • Pack of 3 Le Creuset Firestar Plus refills
**6610** • Firestar burner including one tin of Le Creuset Firestar paste
**6580** • Alcohol Burner
**9112** • White earthenware sectioned Fondue plate

The capacities stated above indicate maximum oil levels.

## GRILLS

**Grillit**
2027.26 — 10 ¼"/26cm

**Round Grill**
2048 — 9" dia./23cm

**Meat Grill**
2049 — 14"x 8"/36x20cm

---

**Giant Grill**
0053 — 18"x 9 ¼"/6x23cm

**Grillomat**
2054 — 9 ½"x 9 ½"/24x24cm

## MULTIPOTS

**Triple Decker**
4191.22
Double boiler 6pt/3.4L
Steamer 8 ⅔"/22cm
Casserole 6pt/3.4L

## STEAMERS

*Enamelled Steel. Fit equivalent sized Traditional Cocottes*

4020.18 — 7 ¼"/18cm
4020.22 — 8 ¾"/22cm
4020.24 — 9 ½"/24cm

## WOKS & STIR FRY PANS

2088.36 — Wok with lid 14"/36cm
2089.36 — Stir Fry 14"/36cm
208804 — Wok Accessory Pack with Shovel, Tempura and Steam Rack

## CHAUDIER

**Table Grill**
6096 — Cast Iron grill plate and stand, Firestar burner. 26cm/10¼"

## DURAMEL RANGE

**Frying Pan**
*Wooden handle*
2408.28 — 11"/28cm

**Skillet**
*Iron handle*
2451.23 — 9"/23cm
2451.26 — 10 ¼"/26cm

**Cassadou**
*Iron handle*
2456.23 — 4pt/2.3L
2456.27 — 6 ½pt/3.7L

**FREE HELPLINE.** IF YOU HAVE ANY QUESTIONS ABOUT LE CREUSET (BEFORE OR AFTER YOU BUY) CALL LE CREUSET FREE - WE WILL BE DELIGHTED TO HELP. DIAL **0800-37-37-92** (MONDAY TO FRIDAY 10 am-4 pm) UK ONLY.

**10 YEAR GUARANTEE.** ALL LE CREUSET PRODUCTS ARE GUARANTEED FOR TEN YEARS AGAINST FAILURES CAUSED BY FAULTY MATERIALS OR WORKMANSHIP. THIS GUARANTEE DOES NOT AFFECT YOUR STATUTORY RIGHTS AND IS VALID FOR TEN YEARS.

**N.B.** SOME COLOUR PHOTOGRAPHS USED IN THIS BOOK INCLUDE LE CREUSET SHAPES WHICH ARE NOT CURRENTLY AVAILABLE IN THE U.K.

# INDEX TO RECIPES